# PARKOUR

and the
## *Art du déplacement*

Vincent Thibault

# PARKOUR

## and the
## *Art du déplacement*
### STRENGTH, DIGNITY, COMMUNITY

Baraka
Books
Montréal

Originally published as *L'Art du déplacement, Force, dignité, partage*
© 2012 Les Éditions du Septentrion
Publié avec l'autorisation des Éditions du Septentrion

Translation © Baraka Books 2013

ISBN 978-1-926824-91-8 pbk; 978-1-926824-95-6 epub; 978-1-926824-96-3 pdf; 978-1-926824-97-0 mobi/kindle

Cover photo: 'Bobby Buildering' by Andy Day
Sketches are by Vincent Thibault
Cover and book design by Folio Infographie

Translated by Casey Roberts

Legal Deposit, 4th quarter 2013

Bibliothèque et Archives nationales du Québec
Library and Archives Canada

Published by Baraka Books of Montreal
6977, rue Lacroix
Montréal, Québec H4E 2V4
Telephone: 514 808-8504
info@barakabooks.com
www.barakabooks.com

Printed and bound in Quebec

Baraka Books acknowledges the generous support of its publishing program from the Société de développement des entreprises culturelles du Québec (SODEC) and the Canada Council for the Arts.

We acknowledge the financial support of the Government of Canada, through the National Translation Program for Book Publishing for our translation activities and through the Canada Book Fund (CBF) for our publishing activities.

Trade Distribution & Returns
Canada and the United States
Independent Publishers Group
1-800-888-4741 (IPG1);
orders@ipgbook.com

# Contents

To Châu, my mentor, friend and brother.

"[In our time], asserting an art of living benevolently—that is, free of all moralism such as the sentimentality of good feelings— is our biggest challenge. Our most necessary as well." *(trans.)*

Fabrice Midal, *La Voie du Chevalier*[1]*

---

* Notes and references may be found at the end of the book.

# Foreword

## By Dan Edwardes
### Director — Parkour Generations and Parkour UK

Parkour is a subject close to my heart. I've been practicing for more than ten years at the time of writing this, coaching for the past seven, and played a small part in helping the discipline spread first across the UK and then around the world. As a physical practice it has dominated my personal training since I discovered it, filling a gap that I was unaware existed in my own development, and as a vehicle for psychological challenge it has pushed me further than I ever thought possible. However, far more important than what it has done for me personally is what I have seen it do for countless others in an endless variety of scenarios and situations.

When we started coaching via our sole class in London in 2005 it was, I believe, the first formal and accessible coaching environment in the world for the discipline of parkour. Prior to this only the French founders—those who had been Yamakasi—provided any teaching and that was to small groups of select students on a somewhat informal basis; a mentorship, almost, which is of course a fantastic way to transmit knowledge.

But mentoring in this way has, unfortunately, a very limited reach. It isn't accessible. And so the benefits and rewards of practicing this incredible art would always be limited to those few individuals fortunate enough to be able to access those founding practitioners in the suburbs of Paris. What we have seen since the opening of the Parkour Generations Academy in London is an explosion of coaching, teaching and involvement across the world that has made parkour arguably the fastest growing physical discipline of the twenty-first century.

It has now touched tens, hundreds of thousands of people across every region of the world, is being offered within schools as a physical education option, utilized in social inclusion programmes for disadvantaged youths, taught to sports education students in universities and even transmitted to professional organizations such as the military, law enforcement, and emergency services. Further, there are now formal, recognized coaching qualifications—the A.D.A.P.T. Programme—created and delivered by many of the founders and principal developers of the art in France and the UK.

These have been broad steps taken by a relatively young and emerging discipline, but this is testament, I think, to one thing: the strength, dedication and resourcefulness of the worldwide community—attributes that are central also to parkour itself.

Books like this one are a part of that. Hopefully a growing part of it, as to date there has been very little of real value published on parkour—a handful of books at best, and many of those in only one language such as David Belle's *Parkour* and Julie Angel's *Cine Parkour*.

But this one adds to that small collection of works of value. It's not a book of 'how-to' but rather an insight into the philosophy of parkour, tackling themes such as freedom, effort, fear, pride, loneliness, courage, humour, and the ever-present social and communal aspects of the art. Which, in a sense, *does* make it a 'how-to'—because parkour is not simply a collection of movement techniques and training methods: it's a concept, an idea, a way of thinking and being. It's an art of living.

Now read on and see why.

# Introduction

This book is an attempt to understand what parkour, *l'art du déplacement*, is and what it can be, and at the same time, both an offering to the discipline's pioneers and a reflection on my own practice. It is aimed at those who, thinking the demanding nature of parkour's exercises are beyond their capabilities, are nevertheless curious, as well as at people who want to learn to move differently, or to find pleasure in new ways of interacting with the objects in the urban environment; at officers of the peace and mayors concerned for our alienated youth; at beginners who are still a bit confused and at experienced practitioners who want to open new perspectives on their art. I address myself to this last group with a good bit of humility, as I still consider myself their student. Some will find my original vocabulary and leaps of thought audacious. But this is only, after all, my own point of view. I'm hoping that everyone—whether experienced or not—will be able to find some inspiration in this book. And I'm dreaming, with a mixture of respect, recognition and pride at what this discipline has to offer, that this book might represent a new point of departure for thinking about parkour. A kind of thinking that leads deeper into life itself.

# Note from
# the Author

**O**ur goal is not to write a history of parkour or launch a debate on terminology.* For some people familiar with the practice, the terms *parkour, l'art du déplacement,* and *freerunning* are not exactly synonymous. For example, it is sometimes said, rightly or wrongly, that parkour's approach is more pragmatic, freerunning's more aesthetic. There are also ideological nuances (motivation, conceptions of sharing, etc.). Of course, both *parkour* and *l'art du déplacement* reflect the French origins of the discipline. *Parkour* is from the French *parcours,* which means route, itinerary, process or path. And *déplacement* is the action of moving from one place to another.

---

* The pioneers of parkour have each their own identity, personality and unique and interesting ideas, and they don't necessarily all use the same terminology to describe their art. Readers who would like to do further research into parkour should refer to *The History of Parkour* and *Ciné Parkour* by Dr. Julie Angel, an independent filmmaker who dedicated her doctoral thesis to this unusual discipline.

In this book, however, we use these three terms interchangeably, with a preference for parkour. In the French text, we liked *l'art du déplacement*, which although encompassing a great deal of territory, seemed perfectly comparable to *martial arts* or *plastic arts.* In the translation, we have mostly used the word "parkour" in an effort to lighten the text. But above all, we hope that the use of these different terms leads to a larger sense of community, since this book is written in the spirit of friendship.

It goes without saying that the sweeping generalizations and romantic side trips contained in this book are the sole responsibility of the author.

# I. Definitions

As your Idea's clear, or else obscure,
Th' Expression follows perfect, or impure

Nicolas Boileau, *The Art of Poetry*[2]

*You're in a city, in an insignificant little space you've seen a thousand times. A small downtown park, a traffic median, a suburban atoll. A concrete forest or a granite beach. You go past it every day on the way home from work, the bus stop is only a few steps further. You go up and down the steps. When you see a tourist delightedly snapping photos, you wonder why. It's just city hall, it's only the post office. The grey annex to a parking structure, the sorry entrance to a non-place, a deserted space that only exists so you can get to another space, perhaps nothing more than a passageway, in any case not a destination in and of itself. Something that punctuates your everyday life without leaving a trace. A bit like the clock you glance at a hundred times a day: who needs to know how it works?*

*One day you encounter a band of urban hominids. A little earlier and you'd have seen them jogging, doing push-ups, practicing the nuances of moving elbows, knees and hips. Warming up, slowly. But now they're gliding, in full flight. They run and leap over a railing with the utmost flexibility, skillfully maneuver up a wall, drop down gracefully and roll on the ground. One of them climbs up the stairs on all fours and then crawls down backwards, his muscular shoulders rippling in the sun. A girl decides to take the ramp: she walks with a sense of balance and assurance you'd expect from a circus tightrope walker. Or maybe a cat. It makes you aware of your animal instincts ... of something primal.*

*The young people are intently focused on what they're doing, smiling from time to time at the encouraging bystanders watching them. Two people walking by think they have chanced upon a performance but quickly realize their mistake: the athletic parkour artists practice the same move five or twenty times over. They're training, learning.*

*It reminds you of a movie chase scene you've seen a thousand times. Crooks and cops, spies and assassins, sprinting and leaping from rooftop to rooftop, exciting, but also disturbing. Is this life imitating art? You kind of hope that they're not playing Spiderman and planning to climb up the sides of that huge office building. Intrigued, you start talking to one of the young participants who's guzzling a bottle of water: he tells you that they are practicing parkour, l'art du déplacement, a discipline where one learns to master three basic skills—running, jumping, and climbing—in all their variants, drawing on the urban environment and the objects within it as inspiration, stage, set, and props. He seems to be able to read your mind: you're obviously not the first person he's seen react with anxiety to what could be seen as a risky and extreme art form. He references the broader culture: action movies are filled with edgy car chases and epic battles of unbelievable violence, but that doesn't mean we can drive without a license or that going to a dojo to study martial arts doesn't also confer health benefits.*

*The metaphor is pleasing. Your eyes are drawn to the background: a parkour artist has just succeeded at doing something that doesn't seem that difficult mechanically, but he has done it with a remarkable degree of precision and grace, with unusual control. He takes two running steps and then jumps, landing silently with both feet on the edge of the sidewalk. He does it again and again.*

*And suddenly, you want to try it yourself! The art of moving from one place to another? At first glance, it just seemed like some young people acting weird, but in fact....*

You might have noticed that the title of this chapter, *Definitions,* is plural. Words enter our vocabulary and derive their meaning from the way they are used by large numbers of people. However, since parkour is a relatively young discipline, there is not always agreement on exact definitions, or even on what language to use. This isn't necessarily a bad thing, since problems can arise when we take ourselves too seriously and we must always guard against becoming too rigid in our thinking. But even though an approach that maintains a healthy mistrust of crystallized ideas can be attractive, it would at the same time be absurd to engage in any kind of practice without really knowing what it was. At the very least, we need to be able to explain to our interested friends what are the elements of a workout that can quickly become so visceral.

I hope to share in this book my personal definition of parkour, *l'art du déplacement*; other practitioners have their own definitions and ways of expressing themselves.

Various disciplines aim to develop our humanity. This purpose is perhaps implied in any artistic endeavour. The martial artist, actor, painter and sculptor share the search for what it means to be truly human; they each wish to sharpen their awareness and to strengthen and refine their understanding of the world. These goals are pretty universal and are shared by everyone who is interested in the meaning of life, whether they be scientists, philosophers or politicians. The difference may be that one of the main resources of the artist is creativity. Creativity—and we will come back to this—is not a goal in and of itself (in the long run, nothing is created just to create, as if we were only interested in production), it is a process of development, a conveyor of meaning.

Countless are the reasons and ways to grow, and none of us is in a position to judge the true motivations of other people.

Parkour, which is both a sport and an art, is no exception: a person might get involved for various reasons, and the benefits to be derived are varied. The best analogy seems to be with martial arts: some people train for self-defense, others to fight (something different); some are looking for health and inner harmony; others see it as a way to express themselves and particularly appreciate the aesthetic. There are still other reasons to train in martial arts, and perhaps it is precisely this diversity that raises this discipline to the level of an *art* and sets it apart from combat sports. One may train in kick-boxing for the competition, or even for health (as long as you don't take too many hits to the head ... but admittedly, the workouts are very demanding). The fact that kick-boxing is a combat sport and not a martial art does not make it an inferior discipline or somehow less interesting, only different.

In fact, there is a wide range of reasons why someone might be attracted by the martial arts. In early adolescence, I had a tendency to look down on people who put everything they had into the competitive kind of training imposed by some contemporary schools of *wushu.*\* Their movements were impressive, imbued with a surprising agility, however, in my mind, they valued aesthetics over efficiency. But even if that were the case, why should I have let that bother me? Maybe it was just their way of growing. I certainly don't claim to know their deepest motivations. Sometimes we believe we can see into the heart of another person, only to find out we're just looking in a mirror that is reflecting back our own doubts and fears.

---

\* *Wushu* is a Mandarin term for martial arts. The reference here is to modern *wushu*, a competitive sport derived from traditional Chinese martial arts.

A similar perspective could be applied to parkour. Some people are initially attracted by the health benefits offered by any balanced training program: rather than building up isolated muscles, parkour conditioning adopts a holistic view of the human body. The exercises are performed to keep the functional anatomy and everything that enables us to fully enjoy the world around us in good shape. The physical preparation takes into account all the muscle groups, tendons, and ligaments, and the healthy relationship that everyone is entitled to have with their own anatomy. This includes their physiology, respiratory system and cardiovascular health; the bone structure and the ways that the impact of certain movements on joints can be reduced (i.e., the precise way of terminating a jump), sense of balance, proprioception, etc.

People also train in parkour for pragmatic reasons: one partial definition of the discipline is to go from point A to point B in the most efficient way (the most efficient, meaning fastest, but also the safest, and if possible, by using less energy). This can definitely come in handy in an emergency. It's not desirable to break a few bones jumping out of a burning building. Just knowing how to "recover" from a serious fall can be, in itself, a very worthwhile skill. Learning how to climb a low wall can also be useful. But training in parkour goes even further, as we have seen. We not only do it to increase our muscle power, but also our flexibility, agility, coordination, sense of balance and to learn to adapt to the environment, regardless of its complexity. The parkour athlete is able to take advantage of ramps and barriers, walls and rocks, façades and railings—and any other supports, surfaces or obstacles he or she encounters. The possible movements and techniques are unlimited.

Having unlimited possibilities does not mean that there are no fundamentals to learn; a certain level of theoretical and practical knowledge is indispensable. This consists of a series of movements that can be broken down and adapted as required (we will see later that adaptability is a key concept). Whether we want to write a novel, essay, travelogue or a children's story, we must first learn to write; we must master spelling, grammar and composition, and then it's up to us how bold or creative we become. This little book is not really a primer in technique, and it's not a way to learn how to perform movements, but a short list of basic techniques seems relevant, at least to situate the reader who has not had any experience in parkour. Experienced readers may wish to skip over this paragraph—with a monkey vault or a precision jump.

To start with, there is the one- or two-handed vault (*passe-ment*), which involves moving past an obstacle (wall, enclosure, table, rock, etc.) that is generally lower than the shoulders of the practitioner. There are a variety of vaults, to gain height, length or speed, and how to perform one is a factor of the entry or exit angle, the proximity of the obstacle, the type of surface, the possibility of placing both hands on the obstacle, the need to get the whole body past it (as in the case where one "fits" between two posts), the presence or absence of a second obstacle with which you can sequence another movement, etc. A wall that is too high to get over with a regular vault is spontaneously climbed using a wall run (*passe-muraille*); you build up some momentum, plant one foot on the wall, gain some speed and height, and use your hands to catch the ridge or the ledge. A *tic-tac* is when you support yourself by putting your foot on an object and push off of it to change direction or to vault over another obstacle. There is also the arm jump (*saut de bras*), where you "hang," usually vertically, by placing your hands on a flat surface (like the top of a brick wall) or else cling (for example, to a post or guard-rail), and touch your feet to the lower part of the obstacle so that your legs can absorb the impact. Precision jumps (*sauts de précision*)

are technical jumps where the goal is to land on a precise surface, usually with your two feet together; running jumps (*sauts de détente*), are performed with a lot of energy and engage the whole body, enabling you to cover the greatest distances. Drops (*sauts de fond*) are made from a significant height (sometimes two meters or more) and are usually followed by a roll (*roulade*), a basic movement that is much more technical than it looks, enabling you to redirect your energy and thereby reduce the impact that otherwise would be absorbed by the body. Some movements involve balance (walking on a narrow surface, advancing "on all fours" on a railing); others require the body to sway (starting, for example, from a position where you are suspended); others depend on fluidity or agility (like thrusting your legs and then the rest of your body through a narrow passage, or sliding under an obstacle).

The approximate definitions in this non-exhaustive list can provide a good idea of the basic techniques. Some practitioners, most of them artists, have come to appreciate parkour as an indispensable way to develop their creativity. Like urban gymnasts or dancers, they slightly vary their basic movements or find new ways of stringing them together, add twists and somersaults and seek elegance in movement. However, to get a good understanding of what parkour *is,* it's important to know what it *is not*: its essence is neither competition nor performance. Parkour is a complete discipline, not to be confused with what young people call tricking or, say, skateboarding or break dancing.* That being said, the aesthetics are sometimes underestimated by beginners. Just look at the pioneers of the discipline in action to see how graceful their movements are. These artistic athletes know that elegance is often a reflection of the control of movement. The aesthetic is not the primary purpose of the practice, but comfort begets

---

* For more on this, see *Parkour and Web 2.0: Make sure not to get caught in the web,* in the appendices.

fluidity, which begets beauty. The pioneers respected the artistic aspect, since *l'art du déplacement* also involves spontaneity, freshness and audacity. Finally—and this is not always obvious to the uninitiated—some exercises that seem *a priori* to have only aesthetic value are very functional (to cite just one example, learning to sense your centre of gravity).

Other practitioners see their art as a means of personal fulfillment. They do it in order to face their fears; to get to know themselves more intimately; to improve in how they relate to other people; to get to the essence of things; to see that obstacles, of whatever kind, are an integral part of life and offer many opportunities for advancement. Parkour is not just a physical discipline, it helps to develop social skills and inner qualities. It leads to—and this book is in good part dedicated to—a sense of universal responsibility and a sense of ethics, a quiet confidence and joy, a practical wisdom. This is the spirit of chivalry in an urban setting. A spiritual path for the modern samurai, but in the service of the heart, not the dictatorship of the ego.

While some young people practice this discipline mainly for the thrill of it, by doing so they are missing the essence of it and tuning out the message of the pioneers. Contrary to the idea conveyed by the media, parkour is not an extreme or elitist sport. Frantically searching for new adrenaline rushes is probably the best way to seriously injure yourself. We will see later how these attitudes—along with those that accompany "feeling too full of yourself"—can be dangerous.

Survival, pleasure, training the mind ... it is essential to periodically review your motivations. For many people, the regular practice of parkour brings about a genuine inner transformation. Our motivations tend to evolve along with our practice, and we'll explore the full range of possibilities further on in the book. One person might be initially attracted by the thrill of the exciting sensations, but a few months later, find him or herself infused with beautiful serenity. Someone else used to get his kicks insulting cops and now tries to befriend them. With eyes finally opened on reality, a surprising sense of magic permeates everyday life.

# II. Redefining Freedom

If we let the hounds of craving, jealousy, arrogance, and resentment run amok in our mind, they will soon take the place over. Conversely, inner freedom is a vast, clear, and serene space that dispels all pain and nourishes all peace. [Being free] means taking one's life into one's own hand, instead of abandoning it to tendencies forged by habit and mental confusion. If a sailor loses the tiller, lets the sails flap in the wind and the boat drift wherever the currents take it, it is not called "freedom" – it is called "drifting." Freedom, here, means taking the helm and sailing toward the chosen destination.

Matthieu Ricard, *Happiness:
A Guide for Developing Life's Most Important Skill*[3]

If we were to randomly ask people for their definition of freedom, we would find that the notion that freedom is the ability to do anything you want, where and when you want, is widespread, especially among young people. Since common sense is not the most universally shared quality, and since people's interests are often in conflict, this kind of "freedom" would surely lead to nothing but chaos and pain. To want to have absolutely any and all desires satisfied—without consideration of other people, the social context or the environment—is typical of children and precisely the opposite of real freedom: we are slaves to the ego and its emotions. Narrow-minded selfishness, jealousy, hatred, obsessive desires, the dictates of a petty tyrant, and all the rest: you might think you're free but the chains are still in place. In a novel by the Japanese writer Haruki Murakami, a character wonders: "What did it mean for a person to be free? Even if you managed to escape from one cage, weren't you just in another, larger one?" [4] It's a good question.

It's easy to imagine what some of the young people who engage in parkour are thinking about when they say they like it for the feeling of "freedom" that it provides. You can jump this way or that way, climb up any wall you encounter and nobody can stop you. You're even in the best position to get away from the cops. It's easy to understand the teenager's desire—a somewhat romantic, if not anarchic, rejection of authority, combined with the (perfectly healthy and legitimate) wish to no longer be constrained by the city, to get on top of it, to love it. It's a way of thinking reminiscent of skate-boarders and participants in other urban sports. But if free-dom and fun sometimes go hand in hand, it's important not to get them confused. Because parkour offers a great deal more than a bunch of adolescent fantasies.

True freedom is above all a state of mind. A mind that is free from disturbing emotions, harmful habits, the comfort of false beliefs, and any and all illusions, especially those relating to one's own identity. People who achieve this state will always be free, no matter the circumstances in which they find themselves. Whether locked up in the darkest tower or tortured nearly to death, they can never be alienated from their true selves. Inner peace, provided it has really become an unshakeable part of who one is, is something that has been painstakingly constructed, not something flimsy or fleeting like an article of clothing that can be easily torn or cast off. The treasures of the heart are the only treasures that can never be stolen.

People who have achieved inner peace are not unfeeling or unresponsive. They still feel sadness, fear and pain, and are capable of reacting to injustice. Just because they are serene doesn't mean they've become machines. They continue to live, act, and interact (of course), only now with more discernment, more consciousness. They draw on their inner strength and commit themselves to abstain from any action that degrades their own humanity, or that of others.

It's not hard to write about, but actually achieving such a state of freedom is the work of an entire lifetime. On the other hand, the quest should not be allowed to become an obsession, otherwise we may remain, in a subtle way, the slave of our desires. This is why we say that the destination is the path itself. Naturally, such a feeling of freedom is accompanied by a better understanding of our own limitations (basic to the practice of parkour), and it is also what is meant by "being free from all illusions, including those relating to our own identity."

This kind of freedom is obviously quite different from the utopian, dysfunctional and dangerous variety in which we actualize our lowest impulses, giving free rein to our desires in the present moment.

With some judicious training (and this has nothing to do with technical competence), parkour can help to develop a sense of inner freedom in relation to a sense of freedom in the world, creating a link between being comfortable with the way our thoughts flow and being comfortable with the way we move our bodies. Parkour mainly involves learning how to move physically, but to move in an efficient, safe, smooth, and if that is your goal, artistic way, you must be in harmony with your environment. First, by knowing its textures, since a hand or a shoe does not react the same way to wood that is wet, stone or steel. We must also respect distances, appreciate volumes, estimate the solidity, density and even resonance of various environmental elements. At its optimal level, this harmony with the surrounding environment is only possible if one is vigilant, patient, open, sensitive and courageous—not qualities of the body but rather of the heart and mind. Hence the link established by this discipline between the two freedoms, inner and outer.

The first necessity is to train your body. Parkour is a strenuous physical practice and you need to give yourself time to prepare your system, at all levels. Your ankle's stability, your shoulder's mobility, your cardio respiratory fitness, the strength of your calves, the muscles in your thighs, stomach, back ... the list is long. This is the most basic protection. Conditioning is challenging, and we explain later how the culture of effort is central to parkour, but it doesn't take long before it becomes its own kind of pleasure. You also gain in strength, endurance, flexibility, balance and coordination ... all qualities that make your body better able to cope with the rigours of existence. This too is a kind of freedom.

After physical conditioning comes technical training. Of course, anyone who knows how to walk knows how to move from one place to another. But we're not limited to one exclusive mode of locomotion: putting one foot in front of the other and moving forward on a familiar surface. It only takes one obstacle—it could be just a puddle, a wall or a garden gate whose key is lost—and we become hesitant and awkward. There are however ways to go even further and with greater confidence. Skilled ways to overcome obstacles, to grow from our encounters with them and to "play" with them, to have fun with them, rather than avoid them. Ways, as we shall see later, to enchant our everyday world and to let our childhood spirit take flight. Especially ways to be more efficient, to avoid being distracted by minor events, to regain our dignity. A healthy human being should not have to fly into a rage when an escalator breaks down.

Even people who don't know how to swim can figure out how to float, at least for a while, if they don't struggle or panic too much. A friend who swims could nevertheless teach us some other methods: movements that can enable you to go faster or swim under water, use less energy, make less noise or to swim on your side in an emergency. Similarly, we can easily walk between our couch and kitchen or between our apartment and the subway station—but we can also learn to run, jump and climb, in the infinite variations offered by the human body, when we are ready to truly enjoy our environment. And knowing that with greater control of our bodies, nothing to prove to others and armed with a whole palette of techniques, we'll be able to take everyday obstacles in stride, contemplate entirely new horizons and change our perspective when the need arises. All this provides a tremendous sense of freedom.

In sum, there is the freedom that comes from knowing that you are worthy and capable.

Of course, true parkour artists are careful not to become too impressed with their own capabilities. The knowledge that they can pass over a 3.6-meter-high wall should not be a source of any more pride than that felt by a fish that knows it can swim upstream.

# III. Finding the Magic in Everyday Life

"It lifts one up," Miss Brodie usually said, passing her hand outwards from her breast towards the class of ten-year-old girls who were listening for the bell which would release them. "Where there is no vision," Miss Brodie had assured them, "the people perish. Eunice, come and do a somersault in order that we may have comic relief."

Muriel Spark, *The Prime of Miss Jean Brodie*[5]

"Children play like rippling water, like the sparkles of the sun, the movements of the clouds. You miss this divine light, which frees the soul and lightens the body. Find this feeling of fullness in all your actions and your life will be transformed."

Dugpa Rimpoché, *Préceptes de vie*[6] (trans. from the French)

Parkour boldly affirms that you can find art anywhere, even in the most unsuspected places; that an original poem can emerge at any time from the banality of everyday living. A moment of inspired creativity can suddenly explode from what seems to be nothing but grey walls and slabs of concrete. Ideally, the parkour artist is a warrior who is intimately aware that beauty is in the eye of the beholder, who is not just an observer, but importantly, an active participant. [*]

Parkour is also the by-product of an encounter, at first tentative and now totally unrestrained, between two spheres of human experience: physical activity and urbanism.

Toronto's Shawn Micallef, author of *Stroll: Psychogeographic Walking Tours of Toronto*, was inspired by psychogeography, a concept developed in the 1950s, which set out to study the effect our environment has on our emotions. [7] Micallef encourages us to let go of our ingrained habits and begin to really explore the city we live in. "The city is never static, it can be perpetually rediscovered." When we open our eyes, we become conscious of thousands of minute details. The author states: "Just by getting off your path, you start seeing the spaces that you pass through differently. Every alley or

---

[*]  It goes without saying that the word "warrior" refers to a man or woman of heart and mind, who commands other assets than violence. We gladly use this image as a tribute to traditional martial arts and the noblest sense of chivalry.

intersection is a new decision, and we end up in parts of the neighbourhood that we didn't know existed."

Micallef does not specifically address parkour or freerunning. He simply invites his readers and fellow citizens to be, shall we say, tourists in their own city, and to draw inspiration from it. It's certainly better than being swallowed up by it.

In any case, psychogeographical walks and parkour converge on this common point: the desire to love differently, to let ourselves be amazed. Audacity, curiosity. However, as pointed out by Dr. Julie Angel, parkour sets itself apart from psychogeographical meanderings by the quality of intention. In other words, the artist of *déplacement* is not just strolling aimlessly. "You set yourself a challenge, one that should be achievable. When you start to attempt it your body gives you instant feedback and you adapt." [8] There is a direction, both literally and figuratively speaking.

*After training for just one week, the small park we spend every day in front of seems to have changed. Like everything else. The driveway, stairs, volumes, textures. We realize that there are dozens of ways to approach the same piece of the city,*

*and that this certain rather horrible concrete structure that made us wonder if it was a failed sculpture or a cage for humans ... well, this concrete structure finally has attracted our curiosity.*

*After a month of training, the same space, the same small park reveals something more. Hidden treasures. The city beautiful reveals her charms, stone by stone, fence by fence, wall by wall. We didn't need to go looking elsewhere—we're in the same space—we only had to open our eyes. Like a woodland hiker who places a hand on a tree to kneel and closely examine a mushroom.*

*After six months, we're sure we've exhausted the possibilities of the small park. We've practiced vaults over the wall, tic-tacs with the rock, and precision jumps between two curbs, countless times.*

*...*

*One morning—after we'd been training for a year—we go back to the park and are delighted to completely rediscover it, to fall in love all over again. We do not know exactly what has happened, no doubt something in the unconscious, but suddenly we realize we are far from having explored all the movement possibilities offered by the park. We decide to enjoy ourselves and spend the entire afternoon there.... At some point, between two jumps, we slow the pace and choose a spot from which we can sit and contemplate the city.*

*The city that had never before seemed to be at once so small and yet so vast.*

Undertaking serious training in parkour changes both how we look at things and how we perceive them. Châu Belle, one of the leading figures in the discipline, explains in the documentary *Génération Yamakasi: Vol au dessus des cités,* "Our awareness of our immediate environment increases. We no longer look only ahead, like some kind of robot, or down at our feet, but also upwards, left and right.... And we begin to see the possibilities that are everywhere." [9] Sébastien Foucan, another pioneer (who has taken a liking to the term "freerunning"), says in the documentary *Jump! London,* "When a bunch of kids pass by a series of small pillars, there is always at least one of them who has to walk on them or jump from one to another. Why have we lost this sense of play, this carefree way of interacting with our world?" [10] Nicolas Bouvier, a traveller and writer and someone who while alive spoke passionately about the qualities of wonder and sharing wrote,

"Childhood, more than being a time of life, is a state of mind."[11] Nothing prevents us from rediscovering this spirit.

It wasn't an accident that parkour developed in the suburbs.* The outskirts of Paris are home to the most diverse

---

\* The French suburban towns of Lisses, Sarcelles and Évry are considered to be the birthplaces of parkour.

physical structures and you can enjoy a wide range of movements. But even more important, for some young people, physical activity became their main way of fighting boredom. Committing themselves to a healthy and rigorous discipline was not just a way of passing time, but a matter of survival. [12] There were other options, and falling into a life of drugs and crime was only too easy. But rather than lead sad lives, bent down under the weight of years of alienation, they decided to see what they—as human beings—were capable of. They are, in their way, great explorers.

Within this framework, teaching parkour could offer an effective solution to the problems of street gangs. Young people, looking out on their world and seeing insipid masses of concrete, could instead discover endless opportunities to develop their artistic talents and to participate in physical activity. By training together, a Turk, an African and a Cambodian generate the possibility of overcoming their separateness; at first only perceiving the subtle differences that set them apart, they could come to discover that they share the richness of their diversity.

As long as they hold strong to their prejudices, members of rival gangs will go on fighting one another; whereas through shared intense effort people who were previously divided can come together based on the simple fact of their shared humanity. Real effort is tangible, and this is the subject of the next chapter.

If practitioners are discerning in how they train, they can enchant the everyday lives of other people and—it's not an exaggeration to say—beautify their city. Later on, we devote a whole chapter to the social skills of the warrior, but it's not hard to see that there's a clear difference between an immature goofball acting out by trashing the urban infrastructure and frightening other people, and a considerate artist who leaves the spaces he or she trains in in immaculate condition and responds in a friendly manner to questions from fascinated observers. It is not a question of putting on a show, but rather of participating in a dynamic of sharing. And when we fall, we're learning about perseverance, rather than showing everybody how violently irritated we can be. You might even say it's the only way to learn. Dignity, respect, drive, elegance, vigilance are all qualities that reinforce each other.

This invites people to see their city in a new way, to become familiar with parkour and to come to respect its devoted practitioners. Who knows? Maybe they will even end up gaining in appreciation for their own bodies, inspired to see what they themselves are capable of.

# IV. For a Culture of Effort

> Two roads diverged in a wood, and I—
> I took the one less traveled by,
> And that has made all the difference.

> Robert Frost, *The Road Not Taken*[13]

**P**arkour is a force to counter inertia. Nowadays, with all the new time-saving technologies and ways of doing things, it is easy to let ourselves fall into expending less and less effort. We live in the automation era, when saving time has become an obsession. Sometimes we even waste time trying to save time. But the question is: how are the couple of seconds gained by the reckless driver who endangers the lives of others actually used? And what about the son who never has time to call his sick mother?

It's certainly more convenient to pay your bills over the Internet than to have to go to the bank and it's also great to be able to instantly send documents to a distant continent or occasionally have Chinese food delivered, but we shouldn't freak out if we can't find the perfect parking spot, or, if we don't happen to have a computer handy, we should (God forbid!) have to write something down by hand. Bruce Lee, in his famous book *The Tao of Jeet Kune Do*, suggested that we park our car a few blocks from our destination, the sole purpose being to make ourselves walk a little bit. And, when possible, to take the stairs rather than the elevator. [14] For your health. For the fun of it. To get in gear. Simply ... out of curiosity.

Some people argue that they are expending effort all the time, that they are already working many more than forty hours a week. But here we can identify two phenomena. In general, we are using our minds more when we work. This can be totally exhausting: our neurons are constantly firing, but our brains don't get enough oxygen. André Van Lysebeth, a great yogi exclaimed: "How many unfortunate pairs of civilized lungs are never thoroughly ventilated." [15] Under such conditions, more or less long-term anxiety and depression are inevitable.

On the one hand, many of us put out intellectual effort almost exclusively, which can be unhealthy—as can be the opposite, that is to say, effort that is physically exhausting, with never a moment to rest or reflect. But on the other hand, whether people work with their brains or their muscles, many of their efforts are only undertaken under duress. The heart is not in it. It is still relatively rare to meet people who are passionate about their work. It's not a question of trying to decide between loving what you do and doing what you love, or to start debating the foundations of modern society. Just ask yourself to what extent the notion of effort is related to the notion of pleasure. We are not always motivated to act by desire, but more often by duty, (which can be quite noble, and is often essential) or by habit, anger or fear. But the fact of having accomplished something in the face of adversity, to have found within our many challenges a source of joy or simply the satisfaction of a job well done, is an experience which is accorded precious little space in our lives. To let ourselves be driven by our old habits, to take things for granted or to constantly complain without ever having to try to find a new perspective can be a particularly vicious form of laziness.

Parkour is a way to counter this lethargy. After all, nobody can force you to buy a pair of running shoes or do sit-ups.

This might be a good time to point out that the effort required to accomplish a given task or exercise differs from one person to another. Think about compulsive workers who can never take a break. For a person like this to learn how to relax might require a surprising amount of determination. In short, effort and ability are related, and this is why training is always individualized in parkour. To fully grasp this, keep in mind that training sessions are often divided into two parts: physical preparation and technical practice, the latter obviously changes every time, depending on the surrounding environment and the available obstacles, the practitioner's level of experience, his or her movement preferences, the training that took place the day before. The real effort here is to repeat the movement and to try to control it, in other words to perform it smoothly and under control as many times as necessary, rather than seeking to get it right one time only. But the physical preparation exercises are totally different from one time to another. We alternate jogging, sprints, all kinds of strength and endurance exercises, forward thrusts, and especially quadrupedal movements (these are the traditional exercises frequently associated with parkour, even though other athletic disciplines also incorporate them). A natural form of training, quadrupedal movement involves moving with three or four "legs" and the movement varieties are endless (crawling like a lizard, hopping like a rabbit, laterally skipping to one side like a monkey, moving with arms and legs extended or folded in, sideways, backwards, in a circle). This has various advantages, including bringing all major muscle groups into play; it avoids impacting the body violently; it teaches us to coordinate breath and movement, and to stay coordinated for the entire activity; it develops proprioception (spatial orientation); it puts us in contact with our immediate environment, awakening our sense of touch and our nerve endings; it's fun, because pleasure is not a bad thing in and of itself and can be experienced almost anywhere; and finally, we can adjust the overall difficulty depending on our energy level—we can create a challenge during every session (i.e., by using gravity, by leaning your body in one direction or another, or simply continuing the exercise over a longer distance).

We practice some of these movements often, but the physical preparation is never exactly the same from one week to the next, as is the case in other sports. We adapt to the environment, and we deliberately vary the exercises. We're not repeating movements just to build up our endurance, but most importantly, to cultivate an enjoyment of effort itself.

One day I went to visit one of my teachers, Lama Lobsang Samten. It was a beautiful summer day, the sun was dancing on the faces of the people walking by. Lama Samten was out on the terrace with his master, Geshe Lobsang Tenpa Rinpoche, a Tibetan monk of the same generation as the Dalai Lama who would later be my teacher. I had come to pay Lama Samten a friendly visit, no doubt intending to ask him a question about some philosophical treatise. But when I joined him on the terrace, I was surprised to find him working on an old piece of plywood furniture. A strike of the hammer, a cut with the saw … He greeted me cheerfully and asked me what I thought of it. I hesitated, before I understood that he was trying to recycle a piece of furniture left out on the street (a neighbour had probably bought a bunch of new office furniture). Discarded or not, Lama seemed to have claimed it, and, without knowing what he had in mind, I started to get into what was going on. His monk's robe made the scene even more touching: he seemed like a young boy taking something apart for the sole purpose of understanding how it worked. We worked up quite a sweat after a number of hours of hard labour under the sun, and finally decided to go inside. In any case, there hadn't been much to save out of the old desk. Once seated inside, my teacher served me a cup of tea and started laughing.

"The furniture's not really the thing. We're working for the fun of it!"

To grasp the role that effort plays in parkour, we must also reflect on the notion of evolution.

Since the dawn of mankind, human beings have always adapted to the outside world. In the documentary *Génération Yamakasi,* Laurent Piemontesi, one of the discipline's pioneers, states unequivocally that the founders do not claim to have "invented" the art of *déplacement.* [16] Running, jumping, climbing: in prehistoric times, humans had to learn to overcome the many obstacles that their natural environment presented to them. Their way of walking improved, they learned to swim, their physiology adapted.

This has been the way of things until very recently in the great human saga. In fact, it was only a few generations ago that a fundamental change took place: rather than adapt to the environment, we now tailor it to suit our desires. In one way of looking at it, this is totally normal, even essential: we can easily build structures to protect us from the elements or make tools to better cultivate the land. But new challenges arise when this perspective outweighs all others. The effort to shape the environment, to the point of exploiting each and every untamed dimension, will inescapably bequeath monumental environmental problems to future generations.

This attitude has serious consequences even on the individual level. People who no longer fit into the urban landscape face the possibility of being swallowed up by the city, suffocated by greyness—physically, emotionally and metaphorically. Especially when only the pathways that have been traced in advance can be perceived, a person can come unconsciously to believe that with such limited options, life is completely predictable, even though in reality life is filled with uncertainties, some for the worse and many for the better. On the roof of an office tower or the crest of a ravine, railings have their *raison d'être*: they preserve the lives of careless tourists and exhausted hikers. It's appropriate to appreciate that these barriers are there and performing their function. But at the same time, practically unnoticeable and insignificant structures that direct our steps and tend to undermine our imaginations have appeared all over the city.[17]

Lawrence Block, an American writer, suggested to aspiring writers that they always take a different path to go home.[18] If we open our minds a little, we can discover dozens of different ways to go to the market or the post office. According to Block, this allows writers to nurture their creativity and helps them to guard against writer's block. If the trick works for writers, who use their imaginations as one of their main working tools, it can certainly be beneficial for everyone else. It's a question of seeing that the world is at the same time both minuscule and immense. That the world is beautiful. Stepping into parkour means to reject being limited to one way of seeing things.

But let's go even further. When we fail to incorporate the objects in the urban environment into our consciousness, we tend to rely on them too much: in the long run, we place too much confidence in external structures, and too little in our own abilities. Of course it's true that a handful of parkour movements involve risks, but if we want to take part in authentic parkour training, we can't be too soft. Minor bruises and a scratch or two are our lot. In fact, the majority of movements are not dangerous per se (at least not any more than, say, in jogging, playing volleyball or any other sport, or even vegging on a sofa, since there are a number of studies that show that prolonged physical inactivity is one of the worst "activities" there is, although that's another story). The human body does seem to be designed to jump, grab, roll, curl, stretch, pull, and push. After a number of weeks, we have already learned, step by step as in all learning, to master some basic movements, which are still perceived as risky by many other people. This reaction is understandable because they are no longer accustomed to moving other than in very specific contexts. However, this fear speaks volumes and the sad fact is we tend to project onto others our lack of confidence in our own motor skills.

How sad is our urban walker, petrified at the sight of a patch of ice! And our noble hero cursing at a rusty old gate that refuses to budge? Would our ancestors really have reacted like this? It's a good question. When we place too much reliance on external conditions, we can easily lose our bearings when conditions change. However, change is inevitable.

Change, evolution.... From this vantage point, we find that training in parkour actually enables us to better appreciate our heritage. First, our animal heritage, by getting in touch with our primal instincts. To train in parkour is to connect with the ancient past. Placing our hand on a tree or on a stone takes on a whole new dimension: in our everyday existence, it's easy to forget that our motor skills are the end result of millions of years of evolutionary development—of mammals, primates and hominids. Some basic parkour techniques are even evocative of other species (monkeys, cats, cranes). But this training also enables us to appreciate the legacy of our human ancestors. In the epic adventures of classical literature, there are passages like: "The good guys departed for the village of X ... and arrived twelve days later." These valiant characters definitely knew something about fatigue. Today, when we want to travel to another continent, we start to seriously stress out if our plane is delayed twenty minutes. To sincerely ask why is in itself a fascinating journey.

We are talking about a culture of effort; in any case we must understand that its benefits go far beyond the athletic context. What we call effort applies to all aspects of life, from the most trivial everyday problems to the most daunting challenges. According to the dictionary, effort is the mobilization, by a conscious being, of all available resources to move past an obstacle, to solve a problem, to achieve a goal or to overcome psychological or environmental resistance. It follows that a person who regularly mobilizes effort and enjoys doing so, at least to some extent; a person who is not too invested in results, as long as he or she gives it everything they've got; someone who knows that one of the highest truths of life is that the process *is* the objective; in short, anyone who embraces the concept of effort will be better able to cope with life's difficulties. An athlete or an artist who has come to be aware of the need to apply themselves in order to succeed and has also learned to relax while doing so might have also realized, for example, that it takes effort and thus sacrifice for an intimate relationship to function smoothly and become established over the long term. When you practice moving forward a couple of hundred meters in quadrupedal movement for a whole week (so challenging you remember telling yourself, "this is going to take as long as it takes, even if I have to spend the entire day doing it"), when you try the same wall pass seventy-five times, when you do as many tic-tacs as it takes to ruin a new pair of shoes ... you've learned something about perseverance, gained in strength, and are now in a position to deal calmly with the small annoyances of everyday life. It's about determination, not about pride. It's about passion.

Passion because sustained effort also enables us—and this is perhaps what has attracted so many people to physical activity—to feel alive. The first time we go hiking in the mountains or perform any other strenuous activity, our muscles are sore for days. Make no mistake: whatever the chosen sport, the first few workouts are often downright painful! However, over weeks, we start to experience genuine pleasure in the effort.

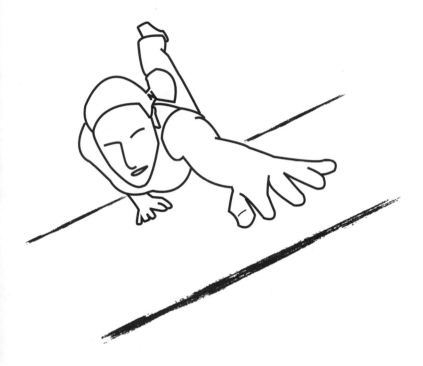

Our blood circulates, our whole body oxygenates, we discover new muscles.... And after the effort comes a well-earned sense of well-being from the flood of endorphins now flowing through our system. There is plenty of evidence and a body of scientific research proving that physical activity helps to prevent and cure stress, anxiety and depression. [19]

A single movement or a few seconds of control may themselves be extremely rewarding. Perhaps because of the effort. The intensity. As a concrete example, there are few movements that require the body to mobilize so many resources as a jump. All the major muscle groups are solicited. We're not just using our legs, even our arms participate. Abs, everything. Imagine that your desired landing spot is relatively far, and that the landing surface is restricted. Something like fifteen centimeters wide. It's far, but with momentum, effort and concentration, you know you can do it. There is nothing quite like the sensation of taking three or four powerful strides and jumping high and far at the same time, and nailing your landing right on your chosen spot. Packed into those few seconds of wonderfully tangible effort is more life than in a whole day spent in front of a computer monitor. Energy flows, effort nourishes. It might be the most sane kind of exuberance there is.

◆

There is so much that could be written on this subject; entire books could be devoted solely to the notion of effort. Our only ambition in this chapter is to open up some possibilities for further thought. However, we want to leave you with one more observation. Effort offers us the possibility of getting to know ourselves better, of discovering our real limits and truly accepting them, in short, to find integrity in an approach that is far removed from obsessing about performance. Effort also draws on our hidden strengths, which are usually over-shadowed by the incessant chatter in our brains. It might seem like nothing but a bunch of nice-sounding words, but to learn more about ourselves is something eminently practical. In a previous chapter, we proposed that parkour can build bridges between our sense of inner and outer freedom. The same sort of thinking applies here. "Knowing your limits" is something to take seriously. Imagine an arm jump (still a jump!) that's been tickling your fancy for a while, say three meters in height. You have to span about four meters, and there's nothing but empty space between here and there, so you have to run, jump powerfully, and finally grab hold of something such as a cornice or a projection, perfectly coordinating the capture by your hands and the damping action of your feet. This is not a jump for beginners. It's possible you saw one of your advanced friends do it, not that that bothers you. You wait patiently for this jump to enter into your circle of "possibles" knowing that it will take the time it takes, and no one will grieve if that moment never comes. Our body is unique, as is our experience, and the city is large and offers us innumerable reasonable challenges. This is just one example, but what it illustrates is that to be unaware of one's limitations could have disastrous consequences.

There is also something very tangible in the idea of hidden strengths. You're out of gas, at the end of your rope, limbs trembling but surrounded by friends, yet you manage another ten or twenty more reps; you've found new breath. Any dedicated athlete has experienced this, and inspiring stories of long-distance runners abound.

But we must nevertheless admit: there really isn't anything else besides what's concrete and what's cement. Because sometimes, through intense effort, our mind suddenly clears. Emptying the body can be a most beneficial experience. We don't want to hurt ourselves, and we're not talking about the unusual idea that it's possible to discover peace of mind simply by working out. We're not trying to be ascetics! But when we are able to discover new resources within us, and when confronted with difficulty we are able to face our fears and thereby understand something of the nature of our egos, windows open. Rigid concepts start to fade, stereotypes and labels peel away. We no longer have a desire to prove something to other people, we are more in the "being" than in the "doing," we are finally ready to welcome existence. Have we ever taken the time to contemplate the beauty of the word "welcome?"

It's a bit reminiscent of what the master Chogyam Trungpa called "going back to square one":

You are slightly sick because you have finally confronted your good old self, but at the same time, you feel slightly relieved because you can still maintain your existence. That type of square one is primordial, rather than imaginary, or a doctrinally conceived idea or concept. It is the really genuine one. Square one should be devoid of any culture. When you're at a low moment of your energy, completely beaten down to the point of death and it feels like you are a piece of shit, you don't feel any culture about that. You feel very genuinely noncultural—and definitely real. [20]

# V. Environment and Social Skills

"There is more to life than good manners; and
politeness is not morality. Yet it is not nothing.
Politeness is a small thing that paves the way for great things."

André Comte-Sponville, *A Short Treatise of the Great Virtues* [21]

"Even in unimportant affairs mistakes come from little
things. One should be mindful of this."

Yamamoto Tsunetomo, *Hagakure* [22]

In some treatises on meditation, whole pages are devoted to the characteristics of the ideal places to retreat in contemplation. Runners, meanwhile, are looking for the ideal conditions for training, for preserving their health, and sometimes to simulate the course of an official marathon. Golfers also pay special attention to the quality of the air and soil, and surfers study the amplitude of waves and the numbers of sharks that are around. Even animals patiently choose where they nest. Is there some reason it should be any different for artists of *déplacement*?

Yes and no. Yes, it's different, as we have seen in previous chapters, insofar as the principles of the practice involve exploring the city (or nature), regaining a sense of freedom, shedding any habits that undermine creativity. This is perhaps what explains the reluctance of some practitioners to see the emergence of dedicated spaces such as skate parks. But neither should it mean running and jumping in any direction whatsoever, without consideration for others, and regardless of the dangers. In fact, with practice, there should be increased vigilance. When training, the responsible practitioner should have taken the time to become familiar with the place; he or she will not linger on someone's property, will inspect the equipment as would any good athlete (that means ensuring the strength of the obstacles to be passed, especially handrails, fences, and anything else that will serve as a support). Out of respect, cemeteries are to be avoided as training spaces, and for safety, places where there are a lot of syringes, or any other unhealthy or dangerous place. An effort should be made to find a balance between places that are too isolated (where there are no resources in case of an accident), and places that are too busy, where there is a risk of disturbing the public. Obviously, you shouldn't waste your time trying to find the ideal place, just use common sense. The range of movements and exercises employed in parkour is huge, you only have to look around and be creative to find innumerable places to train. I remember during an extremely snowy winter looking for some indoor space to rent where a group of us could work out (or even a place I could work out on my own), and the only thing available was the equivalent of an empty classroom. But with the aid of a little creativity I always managed to sweat my fill. Quadrupedal movement, rolls, fun motions using one hand on the ground and the other on the wall, foot placement exercises, precision jumps (by placing strips of tape on the floor), etc. The list is longer than we think. If we can seriously work out in a room practically devoid of any accessory, then people who claim that "their part of the country isn't really that great for practicing," are probably just lacking imagination (or they're not spending enough time on the basics, which is another story).

It goes without saying that a practitioner should show some integrity, for example, by leaving no waste where he or she has been training (water bottles, tissues, etc.). The Yamakasi founders have been working for years to raise the discipline's profile, which has sometimes been tarnished by irresponsible youths. Every citizen should care about the environment, but those who claim to follow a certain code of honour—whether they are parkour artists, martial artists or others—should lead by personal example. Sometimes it is the details that make the difference: pay attention to equipment, which is often part of the public domain; avoid landing in the flowers; if you need to spit, do it discreetly. They are trifles, indeed, but reflect a fundamental idea: parkour is a creative force, not a destructive one. In the world and on the web, you can even see the results of various initiatives of practitioners who have organized themselves as a group to pick up litter. [23] There are countless ways to love your city.

In addition to carefully choosing where you train, an effort must be made to be considerate of people around you. Four groups are deserving of special attention: children, seniors, persons with reduced mobility and street kids.

Children are impressionable. If most adults have lost the ability to wonder, we must not forget that children learn largely through imitation and simulation, but do not always have the capacity for risk assessment. It goes without saying that if a toddler tries to imitate a parkour artist without supervision—particularly when the exercise is done at a height (even one that would not be particularly challenging for an adult practitioner), the risk of injury or even death is real. Although it may be true that the current generation of children is entirely too protected (that is to say too protected from some things and not enough from others), since adults have an annoying habit of projecting their beliefs and anxieties onto their offspring, it is simply a fact of development that these little persons absolutely must explore their world! Children have a natural desire to move that should not be stifled; with proper guidance, it is even quite possible for them to learn parkour. In any event, the goal here is not to talk about how to raise kids, but rather to encourage practitioners to keep their eyes open while training in front of children who have been left unsupervised.

More than a few seniors are fascinated by urban acrobatics. Some applaud or make jokes about their own physical condition, some even express the desire to learn. We don't have to stop practicing just because some members of a neighbourhood association are playing bocce. We do need to be careful, however, when we practice *sauts de fond* (dropping from a significant height, say two meters or more). Falling out of the sky and landing right in front of some person with heart problems could end badly. Heart problems or not, we need to at least watch out for drivers who might be momentarily startled and lose control of their vehicles.

When parkour artists encounter people with reduced mobility, a little compassion and intelligent relating goes a long way. What we're doing may unintentionally throw the fact of their disabilities right in their faces: "Here is what we are capable of doing, but not you." In fact, few people will have that reaction, but it's still a question of being tactful. When we are sprinting, deep in the thick of the action, darting down unusual city pathways, we need to remember that not everyone has quick reflexes and the ability to avoid fast moving objects.

Many street youth amiably share their world with urban athletes. As Yamakasi cofounder Yann Hnautra explains, artists of *déplacement* create links between institutions and people alienated from them, between rich and poor, between different ethnic groups, between young and old. [24] According to David Belle, urban gangs are nothing to be afraid of, if one has peace of mind and is sincere: "When the inner city guys meet up with a parkour group at night, they receive a lot of energy, they see other young people having fun doing vaults, doing moves, encouraging each other. They understand that these people are not out to give them a hard time. They're just using the architecture. Attitude is important in parkour: when we know where we're going, nothing bad happens to us." [25]

A number of young people living on the edge are attracted by our atypical practice; skateboarding and break dancing are a familiar part of their culture. There's nothing wrong with them joining in, quite the contrary. However, one thing should be kept in mind. Without being too judgmental and especially without generalizing, be aware that some itinerants consume a surprising amount of drugs and alcohol and sometimes become overexcited or too aggressive in their first attempts at parkour. So be responsible and be a model. We're not sitting in judgment here; in any case, we can't really know the true reasons why people do what they do and there's sometimes more wisdom in the street than we realize. But we must develop one basic communication skill: adapting to the other person. Adaptability is the essence of parkour. It is also a basic principle in education. And if it's accomplished with love and

integrity, it becomes the best potting soil in which to germin-
ate lasting friendships.

Whatever might be said about it, parkour is a young discipline
and it is the responsibility of practitioners to demonstrate
maturity and anticipate and avoid problems that could arise.
The most effective way to do so is not to imagine every possible scenario, but rather to focus on core values, especially
respect and integrity. Earlier we discussed respect for others,
and the elements touched on in this chapter make good sense.
But it is also essential to respect yourself, to move towards
true freedom and empowerment. We need to be careful not
to impose what we do on other people, but neither should we
feel like we have to stay out of sight.

# VI. Facing Fears

"Wholeheartedness is a precious gift, but no one can actually give it to you. You have to find the path that has heart and then walk it impeccably. In doing that, you again and again encounter your own uptightness, your own headaches, your own falling flat on your face. But in wholeheartedly practicing and wholeheartedly following that path, this inconvenience is not an obstacle. It's simply a certain texture of life, a certain energy of life."

Pema Chödrön, *The Wisdom of No Escape* [26]

In the documentary *Jump! London*, Sébastien Foucan notes that the same fears people experience in parkour training are also present in everyday life. [27] Our discipline—which is called *l'art du déplacement*, freerunning or parkour—provides a workspace, a way to make friends with our fears, to come to know our personal limitations, to explore their textures and experience their rationale.

The general practice is to try to escape from fear, to flee anything that we believe will affect our fragile equilibrium, to stay all wrapped up in the comfort of familiarity. It is normal to want to avoid pain and to seek happiness, it is a principle at the basis of all life (i.e., survival). But to achieve true happiness, and not an artificial or ephemeral substitute, we need insight. And insight is only possible if we stop running away. Everyone has days when they want to stay home tucked under the blankets, but we can't spend our entire lives doing that. We must abandon our false, albeit comforting, beliefs. We need to face the world. Experience the world.

When we say that parkour enables us to face our fears, people almost invariably think we mean fears such as the fear of heights or the fear of falling. But working at a height is just one of the many different aspects of the discipline, and there are a number of different kinds of fears that can come up in the course of this practice. There is the fear of losing control (of the situation, the immediate environment, but especially of yourself, physically and psychologically); fear of loneliness, ridicule or shame; fear of the unknown, weakness, injury, death or oblivion, disease and aging. Parkour is an extremely demanding challenge, but one that can enable us to examine each of these fears, to look into our minds with all the honesty we can muster—the key to becoming truly human. It is not, strictly speaking, a question of toughness, as in "I can tough it out—this fear, this discomfort—and I can handle my ever-growing pain." What we really need to do is to learn how to identify which fears are our friends, and how others hold us back by deforming our perspective of reality. A widespread misunderstanding, especially among young practitioners, is that the purpose of parkour should be to eliminate all our fears. As if they were trying to emulate Wolverine in attack mode, Asterix flush on magic potion or Son Goku at the peak of his form. Evolve to the point where you have nothing to fear and can jump from building to building, roll around on concrete, slide over rocks, cling to steel, bounce off of bricks, surmount any challenge, at any speed and at any height. Can you absolutely pulverize all your fears out of existence ... really? Unless you've become a total robot, it would be impossible; in any case, it's not desirable. Many fears have their uses, their rationale, and to study how they function is actually quite fascinating.

One of the best books on the subject, which reads like a novel, is the essay by Christophe André entitled *Psychologie de la peur: Craintes, angoisses et phobies*, published by Odile

Jacob. Throughout the book, the author reminds us how fears can be beneficial and essential: "Fear acts as an alarm, whose function, like all warning signs, is to draw our attention to danger, to enable us to deal with it. The problem is that our alarms can be set to be more or less sensitive." *(trans.)* [28]

And it's up to each of us to know where to set our own alarms. It's up to each of us to be good students, to live well:

nothing can force us to grow in self-awareness. Sometimes we need to experience fear. This is also true of parkour: to experience our fears, break their stranglehold (or to sometimes fail to do so) and not to run away from them, forget about them or deny them. We have to be able to dig down deep and avoid swallowing our fears just for other people's entertainment. We have to move forward, rush on ahead, slow down to find our balance, come to a stop and gather ourselves, sometimes even step back in order to generate some momentum or to see the big picture. This is very concrete, a way to come in contact with reality. Before, during and after training, all sorts of things can go through your head ... it's up to you to sort it all out. We must properly honour the fears that keep us alive and push us to improve, and shed the ones that hold us back.

Of course, you don't need to jump from the thirtieth floor of a building in order to do this. But if you can perfectly execute a movement one foot off the ground, it's perfectly logical to wonder why you shouldn't just go ahead and try it ten feet up? I did three thousand precision jumps landing on a round bar barely off the ground and never fell; why should I be afraid to do the same thing at a height of three meters considering that the jump is shorter and the surface I'm going to be landing on is ten times larger? * There's no denying that the risk of injury is greater if you fall from a height, but it's an interesting question nonetheless. At what point does the mind influence the quality of our movements? There are times when fear pushes us to be more vigilant, so as to succeed; other times, our anxieties cause us to fail to execute. We've all experienced this, especially in the first months of training (because after a while, the mind tends to change): we start to take a movement that we have deftly executed many times for granted, but it only takes one miss and the accompanying pain to shatter our confidence and then weeks of further effort before being able to graciously perform the same movement again. It's a question of being blocked mentally, not a lack of technical knowledge or physical ability. We come back to the same question: at what point does the mind influence how we move?

Regardless of the situation, it remains true that we have to get rid of the fear of being afraid. The formula sounds trivial, but what it expresses is unimaginably profound. Don't push fear away, rather, welcome it. If you look at it more closely, that could be the very definition of the word "courage."

---

\* Obviously, before trying any such jumps we learn how to recover from a fall, sharpen our reflexes, train our bodies for a considerable period of time, completely master the roll, etc.

# VII. Ego Traps

"All those who suffer in the world do so because of their desire for their own happiness. All those happy in the world are so because of their desire for the happiness of others.

Why say more? Observe this distinction: between the fool who longs for his own advantage and the sage who acts for the advantage of others."

Shantideva, *Bodhicaryavatara*[29]

In the previous chapter, we saw how fear wears many faces. In fact, the same masks often adorn the ego in its effort to get noticed: the armoured carapace and thick shells which tend to promote the illusion that our selves are immutable, and inevitably like this or like that. Our little egos can be incredibly deceitful in assuring themselves that they exist. I'm Lenny Spartacus, I'm 28, I can do the most awesome wall run in the city, I'm the only one to have nailed a certain arm jump, I can run faster than most superheroes (and besides I am one), but deep down I'm really scared of getting old. I'm Vincent

Thibault, I write books, so I must be pretty intelligent, the work I do is definitely important, and I deserve some recognition. The ego tends to distort the way we see ourselves and justify what we do.

It is not always easy to identify this kind of distortion, and its effects vary greatly in severity. Here's a simple example. Sometimes we feel as though we're simply too tired to continue training. But is it really true, or is something else going on? Is there a real physical need—and a key protective mechanism kicking in—or just some well-camouflaged laziness? Are we afraid of failing to execute a supposedly simple movement in front of bystanders or other practitioners? Are we lacking confidence in our abilities? If we stop would that show there's a pattern of not putting out enough effort? Asking yourself these questions can be a challenging exercise, but real training involves learning not to deceive ourselves. Authenticity is one of the main qualities of the warrior.

At worst, by feigning fatigue or amping up any small loss of energy, we withdraw from action; even if inactivity becomes a habit, the only damage we risk is that we stop learning—unless this lethargy starts to manifest itself in all aspects of our lives. What's even more problematic is to become deliberately oppositional: to refuse to listen to our body, to turn a deaf ear to its warning signals and its desperate need of rest. Often, this kind of neglect or incorrect assessment is itself the result of a hardened ego. "I exist," "I am strong," "I can do it." "I'm not weak, get it?" If we attempt to tease out the underlying meaning of a great deal of everyday conversation, we realize with astonishment that these short little statements are what people are basically saying. But obsession with performance is even more dangerous when practicing a sport or discipline that involves risk. That being said, the risks found in parkour are not inherent in the discipline itself; the degree of risk is the practitioner's choice. He or she is responsible for exercising discretion and humility. Of course, even people who do not practice sports are regularly confronted by hazards and a degree of uncertainty, whether they're conscious of it or not. The parkour artist's task is to determine which risks, even those that are carefully calculated, facilitate growth, and which others only cater to the ego (the exact opposite of growth).

We are living through a moment in history where performance has assumed the highest value. The notions of pleasure, serenity, sharing and compassion seem totally insignificant in the context of market research or geopolitical strategy. Only results matter, yet we have become accustomed to validating what is tangible and precisely quantifiable. But there are many things whose value cannot be calculated: determination, desire, patience, the ability to cope with the vagaries of life, a child's smile, a sick person's final moments, the betrayal of a loved one, genuine friendship, the flavour of an exotic fruit, the quiet joy of a walk in the country or the contemplation of a sunset. The solution is not to be found in running after every new development in pop psychology or new-age spirituality, but rather to stay in balance and separate fantasy from reality. Metrics are useful to us and that is what we mean by tools: by definition, tools are not the whole picture, they must serve a greater cause. We can use tools to create other tools, but only temporarily, otherwise the principle of production becomes sterile and everyone suffers.

This digression is less elusive than it might seem. In parkour, people who never evaluate distances are guaranteed to hurt themselves. But those who overcalculate get injured too. Take the case of someone who measures the length of a precision jump between two walls down to the centimeter. He no longer trusts his instincts and has lost spontaneity—an essential faculty, since some factors are unpredictable and uncontrollable. He's stiff. His intellect is working so hard that he inevitably forgets to take this or that detail into account.

Technique. Height. Width. The angle. Strength. Speed. The wind. Moisture. Fatigue. Stress. The grip of his shoes. The flight of a bird, the cry of a child, the reflection of the sun.

Simply calculating is one thing. Even more dangerous is to set your sights exclusively on measurable achievements. To obsess over results. To reach for a new record. Parkour artists must break with the frantic performance drive instilled by the modern world. They are among the best placed to know that we all have different sensitivities, physiologies, capabilities, and goals. Of course, some people develop exceptional abilities through disciplined training. But these faculties are developed over time, and we must never forget that the benefits of training are also acquired during periods of rest. Parkour requires progressive training, because even with good technique and after weeks of conditioning, the body is still not able to perform certain movements (tendons and ligaments, to give just one example, do not grow at the same rate as muscles).

A friend wanted to learn parkour from one of the discipline's pioneers, a member of the Yamakasi group in France. His mentor tasked him to only perform preparedness and conditioning exercises for a full year before he would teach him any techniques. Our man persevered, and it was not in vain: he achieved technical mastery with surprising speed (his body could enjoy the movements and not just endure them, and his mind had become used to providing real effort). Today he is a very talented practitioner, a highly esteemed instructor at the Yamakasi ADD Academy. The story is reminiscent of the stories of legendary martial arts masters of old.

"How long do I have to practice to reach enlightenment?" a young monk asked the Zen master.

"Well," he answered, in a half-playful half-serious tone, "let's say twenty years."

"Twenty years!" exclaimed the young man. "And if I'm in a hurry?"

"In that case, forty."

Undoubtedly, many injuries—fractures, lacerations, etc.—are the result of the ego's tyranny. Even without needing to prove something to other people, we are sometimes driven to prove something to ourselves. This can be a particularly perverse form of neglect and, in the long run, damaging to the body. We have a tendency to seek immediate results in different spheres of living and we often try with all our might to become somebody. Playing the comparison game is easy, as is putting people up on pedestals. But even if it is something quite different to draw inspiration from mentors, and even if our contact with them can be humbling—when we see how skilled they are, for example—we can also lose sight of our personal limits and impatiently throw ourselves into overly difficult challenges if we forget that these same mentors have acquired their skills over time. To see, for example, the speed and raw power with which Yann Hnautra or David Belle can come down a building will reinvigorate an enthusiast. We should remember, however, that Yann and David have been training all their lives.

In the same way we might misunderstand the concept of personal growth and have a need to revise our definition of development: the goal is not to become someone else, but to learn to be genuinely ourselves.

The art of *déplacement* is a gateway to authenticity. I remember a seminar in Columbus, Ohio.[30] Three days of intensive learning and training. On the afternoon of the last day, many of us had a chance to study with Benoit Odoyer, an instructor from the ADD Academy, who had come from France for the seminar. After a rather tiring day, he invited us to "relax" and let our creativity take flight. Try out some original sequences, show some spontaneity. Discover, adapt. At the end of this unusual training session, he insisted that we all sit down for a moment and share our experiences. Patiently, he explained how important it was for each person to bring their personal heritage into their practice. He said, and I'm paraphrasing: Do not deny who you are, honour your past, and do not build your future simply on dreams. Whether you come from martial arts, dance, yoga, or any other field, your previous experiences have made you who you are. Practicing parkour does not require you to forget who you are. There are specific basics to learn, but we should not feel compelled to incorporate every move somebody has done and called it "parkour" or "freerunning." Find the middle way: enjoy and bring your own kind of energy (and yes, find your own way to move and express yourself), but parkour is *not* gymnastics or capoeira, etc.

Two months later, I returned to Columbus, this time for a certification course run by Dan Edwardes, director of Parkour Generations, who had come from England for the occasion. Dan spoke to us at length about the importance of staying

within yourself, of the grace and strength that underlie profound integrity. It was an inspiring moment for everyone.

Practicing parkour in public: falling, getting up, doing it over
and over again without getting discouraged, helps counter-
balance people's prejudices. It becomes easier for other people
to understand the concept of training, experimenting,
expending genuine effort. If Person A sees Person B awk-
wardly trying some acrobatic stunt before continuing on his
way, hoping that no one saw him fall, Person A will think it
was nothing more than a whim, a moment of craziness perhaps. But if Person A sees someone attempting a jump, once,
twice, twenty times, each time striving for more precision,
fluidity, efficiency and control, Person A will understand that
Person B is training.

It is natural to fall, to fail to execute a movement, no matter
what level of mastery we've achieved. The concept of training—of apprenticeship—is fundamental to learning: progress-
ing from what we know to what we don't, which immediately
implies estimating, trying, and erring. No one learns to ride a
bike without a bit of hesitation. To get down on ourselves at

every failure is to condemn ourselves to permanent incompetence. Being arrogant is the surest way not to learn. Because everyone knows that to learn anything we must (once again) accept that we don't know (something).

Even when you're totally alone, humility is one of the most powerful learning vectors (we are talking about a well-proportioned humility, not a lack of confidence in your abilities). Many young practitioners strive for speed, height and length. In short, performance, achievement. They're not really zoned in on the details. Yet what we recognize in the established practitioners is their finesse; they don't land like elephants, they seem to effortlessly string together different movements and don't waste any energy doing it. Imagine someone moving with fluidity between two railings, practicing a lazy vault over a ramp, taking three strides that seem perfectly calculated (and yet instinctive) before executing a precision jump over a rock; landing on a wall and then descending without a pause in a natural movement followed by a roll—all without making a sound—getting up without interrupting her forward motion the least bit, jogging to the next obstacle and handling it with maximum efficiency, that is to say, using just the right amount of strength. And there she is, doing the sequence over and over again. If we observe veteran practitioners working out for a period of time, we'll notice that many of them are content with very simple movements. An interesting analogy can be made with yoga: the covers of yoga magazines often showcase preposterous contortions, sometimes demonstrated not by yogis but by models whose job it is to be flexible, even though the masters have been satisfied over the centuries with positions that seem commonplace.

So when you're training, it is better to learn how to master each movement, rather than trying to quickly reach certain milestones of height or speed. The advice of the pioneers is to first slow the movement down until you're comfortable with it, and move through the three stages of learning in a logical order: do it, do it well, do it quickly and well.

We said earlier that to learn, we must face up to the fact that we still don't know. This is reminiscent of one of the teachings of Zen master Shunryu Suzuki that we might reflect on again and again:

"In the beginner's mind there are many possibilities, but in the expert's there are few." [31]

# VIII. To Be and to Last

> "[A word of caution at the beginning of the book:]
> Warning: Before beginning a program of physical
> inactivity, consult your doctor. Sedentary living is
> abnormal and dangerous to your health."
>
> Frank Forencich, *Exuberant Animal:*
> *The Power of Health, Play and Joyful Movement* [32]

At this point, it would be good to review some of the concepts we have already touched on. We have so far reflected on inner freedom and freedom of movement, creativity and the magic of everyday life, effort, and once again, effort, the environment and social skills, fears that are our friends and fears that hold us back, the ego that tends to show up wherever we are. Now, we are going to talk about health.

When people hear about parkour, the first thing that many of them think of is that this is a highly dangerous practice. One of the main goals of this book is to prove that parkour is not an extreme or elitist sport. Let's not be naive: to many young people around the world, it is an extreme sport, and some even practice a questionable mixture that draws from parkour (a discipline) and the moves done by a cinematic stuntman (a trade), adding a little of this, a little of that. But in essence, parkour simply means better control of basic skills—and the adjective "basic" could be considered to be the antonym of "extreme." Anyone who invests the effort will get something out of it. Anyone who still commands their motor skills can learn to move in a different way, and appreciate doing the sometimes fun exercises that comprise training. To alternate jogging, plyometric exercises, all kinds of ways of moving on all fours, balance, agility and coordination exercises is anything but boring; and anyone looking for a different, natural, adaptable training method that requires no special equipment will be satisfied. Physical education teachers, government health ministers, sociologists and doctors all try to entice people to lead more active lifestyles. Parkour could provide a solution. It is so simple, so effective, so fundamental, it inevitably reminds us of the tree that hides the forest and all the things that are too close to our eyes to be fully appreciable.

In fact, health should be the cornerstone of our parkour practice. Among the slogans of the founders we find the phrase "to be and to last." The only way to establish a long-term practice is to take care of our bodies and be vigilant in training. Of course, we should not idealize the practice; we earlier spoke about the culture of effort, and it goes without saying that if your idea of a good time is to go whizzing within inches of the ground, brick, cement or stone, scratches, bruises and small cuts are sure to follow. But the risk of serious injury, though not completely absent, is lower than you think—at least, for anyone who trains with discernment. The essence of practice should be to get to know your limits. Repeat a movement as many times as necessary: it is not a sport where success is measured by how many goals we've scored, or a discipline where speed prevails. Since we are movement artists, we move to find out who we are. We are in search of harmony and peace.

It follows that in order to better manage their health, practitioners use a range of methods, and it is the same for any serious athletic activity: maintain a healthy balance between fitness and technical practice, overall and progressive conditioning, while taking into account personal objectives, preparations, warm-ups, stretching, relaxation periods, rest days, a healthy diet and adequate sleep. To which we could add two frequently omitted points: a basic understanding of human anatomy and physiology and friendly relations and exchanges with peers.

However, even though we can try to reduce the risks, we're always vulnerable, and injuries can indeed occur (and they are as varied as are the movements in parkour). However, we can learn a lot from injuries; they offer us a space from which we can gain new perspectives, and the time we spend healing allows us to recharge our energy stores and to reflect on how we are training. For many, it is an opportunity to deepen their theoretical understanding of the movements, to learn about the human body and health, to sharpen their observational skills, to look within and find some quiet, some balance. Following a serious accident, Bruce Lee found himself bedridden for several months. He took the opportunity to write down his thoughts on his art, and the relationship between it and the wisdom of the East. These writings and sketches, later collected by his wife, became the subject of a book, *Tao of Jeet Kune Do*, which no doubt has already carved out a place for itself in the history of world philosophical literature and remains one of the best references there is on all the different varieties of martial arts.

But one of the best lessons that an injury can teach us is to encourage us to think about what caused it. The documentary

*Parkour: The Nature of Challenge* reveals an important point: a fall or an injury does not imply a personal and total failure, as if our person had no value; rather, we usually fail as a result of an incorrect assessment of the situation. [33] This is very much a matter of observation, vigilance, and knowledge of the environment and, especially, ourselves. We discussed in the previous chapters other possible causes, including arrogance, lack of physical preparation and poor understanding of the essence of the discipline. It may also be as a result of being too much in your head when moving or, on the other hand, to have your mind elsewhere at the time of execution. This is reminiscent of the Buddha's teaching: when discussing the best way to meditate, he gives the image of a string on a musical instrument, which must be fine tuned to be "neither too tight nor too loose." This is true for how the mind must be balanced, and it is also true for physical balance and ease of movement. Even in architecture, we know that if the most rigid materials are positioned in the wrong place, they are likely to be less effective or literally break.

An injury can also be caused by poorly managed enthusiasm. We want to go too high, too far, too fast. Or we become fascinated by one aspect of the practice to the neglect of others and the whole suffers from an imbalance. Or we work too hard and become a good candidate for overtraining and the undesirable consequences that tend to accompany this phenomenon.

These points have been made many times before. Anyone with the slightest interest in sports has already received plenty of advice on this subject. But a simple idea that is seldom discussed—and this omission speaks to our lack of understanding of health and "exercises" that "must" be done—is the notion of pleasure. At first glance it doesn't seem that complicated: try not to make your workouts overly grim, vary the exercises so as to work the whole body and avoid monotony, take things with a bit of humour without detracting from the seriousness or depth of your approach, make sure to allow yourself some relaxing breaks, be playful, challenge yourself. By the way—is it necessary to be reminded?—when we talk about challenges, we have the childlike love of discovery in mind and not the over intense competitive spirit that is truly foreign to parkour.

It's a sad fact that when we talk about "lifestyles" these days, we rarely mention joy. We want to be "healthy" and we need to lose weight, build up lean mass, look good, even if appearance counts for little, maybe our doctor has put us on a strict exercise program, or we've fallen into the clutches of a Spartan

coach. So we go to a gym, or how about a centre, or an insti-
tute? Monday and Wednesday, and sometimes on Sunday, we
strictly time ourselves, we speak of "repetitions," "sets," "kms,"
"pulse," "number of hours per week." But all the while, we
forget to have fun. We've just made one of the biggest mistakes
of modern life in terms of health: to echo Frank Forencich,
we've made movement into a specialty, confined to a particular place at a particular time. [34] We've frozen even the concept
of movement, turning it into its opposite, into something
outside ourselves and constraining, when it should be a basic
act of freedom, a creative force. But movement is not a specialty, a duty, or a good idea that you can put on the shelf, it's
a way of life. Life is movement.

Keep pumping those free weights if that's what really rings
your bells. But have we forgotten that laughter is a great way
to work a surprising number of muscles? Well, there I'm over-
reaching. In any case it's pretty reductionist to think only of
muscles when meditating on the benefits of pleasure. Parkour
is an inexhaustible source of fun—and gratification. This is
equally true for beginners and the more advanced, true for
adults, teens, and young children alike. [35]

◆

In Forencich's fascinating book *Exuberant Animal: The Power of Health, Play and Joyful Movement*, the author explores the ideal "program" of physical activity for humans, drawing parallels with the main types of motor locomotion of other animals. It's worth summarizing his compelling rationale. This will allow us to better understand how exercise "programs" are sometimes counter-productive, if not downright unhealthy.

Motor abilities developed in relation to animals' preferred eating habits, so we can identify three main types of schemes that are associated with fundamental movement patterns: herbivore, carnivore and omnivore.

Herbivorous food is so poor that the animals must graze constantly. Eat a few blades of grass, move a bit, a few leaves, move a little. Except for occasional outbreaks of playful activity, mating and responding to the sudden attack of a predator, physical activity is usually minimal.

Carnivores are striking contrasts. The meat they eat is so rich, they can spend several days digesting it. They aren't too active during this period; we've all seen pictures of lions basking in the shade all the livelong day. But when hungry, the carnivore's level of physical activity goes off the chart. The lion may bask, but after a day or two ... poor antelope!

Omnivores eat such a variety of foods that they must master a wide range of motion to acquire it. A primate uses all its members and can just as easily find a meal on the ground as munch a snack at the top of a tree. In fact, as Frank Forencich points out, a large part of the lives of omnivores is devoted to exploring and seeking new opportunities.

Biologically, human beings find themselves among the omnivores. But many people adopt an "herbivorous program" (obviously we're not speaking here of vegetarianism): a continual flow of low-intensity physical activities (studying, talking, driving the car, answering e-mails, printing documents, watching TV) punctuated by an unlimited variety of stimulants (beverages of all kinds, snacks and meals on the go that are low in essential nutrients). Others take a carnivorous approach in terms of physical activity: their program consists of very intense training sessions, all followed by an incredible gurgitation of food and then a long rest, sometimes spanning several days. But whether it's a fully developed lifestyle in which any form of movement has been banished (consciously or not), or just everyday behaviour that lurches between the extremes of absolute performance and allegedly regenerative apathy, none of this seems to be in synch with our biological heritage. It is imperative that we find a balance: a way of life where we can enjoy all kinds of movements on a regular basis.

According to Frank Forencich:

> The opportunistic program suits not only our bodies, but our temperament as well. Being generally sapient, we enjoy a diversity of challenges. We like movement of all varieties and we like to mix it up. The herbivore program bores us, as well it should. The predator program excites us, but the spikes come too far apart for our taste. Our bodies and our minds thrive on frequent movement of all kinds. Diversity contributes to sustainability which, in turn, contributes to psychophysical health. [36]

This seems to be an excellent subject for both the individual and the community to think about.

If our injuries offer us many opportunities to reflect on their causes, it would be absurd not to spend some time thinking about their effects. In a way that is similar to how we contemplate the past so that we might better anticipate the future:

meditating on health can help us to refine our understanding of our vulnerability and vice versa. In short: injuries give us the opportunity to reflect on what constitutes true strength.

I remember a conversation with Chau Belle, a founding member of Yamakasi. We were in a café in Paris, and he told me about an injury he had suffered and how he had to work twice as hard to regain his initial rhythm. At one point, he leaned closer to me:

"If you break a toe, that's one thing. But if they have to amputate your arm tomorrow, how will you be strong? And if you lose your legs? What does it really mean, to be strong? You know, sometimes you have to think about it."

It seems that our concept of strength is often simply based on the idea of physical performance. But with a little thought, it becomes clear that when it comes to strength, what predominates is determination, courage and presence of mind and heart. It's strange but true: we often consider the proud strong and the stubborn mighty, when what they are revealing is precisely their weakness. Recognizing one's own vulnerability and keeping one's personal limits in perspective are sometimes signs of the most authentic mastery, true strength.

# IX. Alone in the Jump

"We start together, we finish together."

One of the precepts of the ADD Academy [37]

"Do not be afraid of solitude when it comes your way. It's an opportunity to find yourself and strengthen yourself."

Dugpa Rimpoche, *Préceptes de vie* (trans.) [38]

The previous chapter ended with a beginning, the beginning of a new way of thinking about true strength. This way of thinking is new because we've already dipped our toes into the subject of strength: freedom, the culture of effort, ego traps; all topics that are related to courage, which we will talk about again in the next chapter. Dizzying refrain; you'd think you need a bit of courage to be ... brave. Everyone in favour, raise your hands! Everybody else? Take a lap!

No, it doesn't work that way. You do not grind out yet another lap alone. At least not at the ADD Academy, where one of the fundamental values that is taught is team spirit. It is together that we are really able to gain in strength. By myself, I lift weights; together, we raise the sky. Parkour practitioners are an inexhaustible source of energy to their friends. Sharing is fundamental to the practice; otherwise the whole process quickly becomes sterile.

There are many reasons for this. We provide encouragement to each other, through words and through our presence; showing by example, breathing together and sharing our effort. We never leave someone crumpled on the asphalt, exhausted, baked. Those who feel particularly strong on a given day start the exercise, accompanying those who are exhausted during the last meters of quadrupedal movement. "We start together, we finish together, one heart, one crew." we chant during our workout, like the congregation responding to a call and response. We're a team and we help each other: the formula might sound childlike, but why should it? Annoyance is given no space to flourish, because whoever really adheres to the precept discovers an unimaginable pleasure, the feeling at the same time of being supported by others and being useful to them; the image catalyzes learning and is a source of joy, that undeniable intangible in healing. In sum, we have found a family, and a loving family at that. The training sessions feel safer; a brother or a sister is never far away.

Finally, as we have already said, a group that trains in public, and with proper respect, is a creative force in the city. It's a way to project the inherent dynamism of the discipline onto the rest of society.

There's energy in sharing. A good example is the exercise where thirty people move on all fours. Sometimes, however, there's just a handful of practitioners, and they're training in one of the less busy spaces. Even then, there is cause for celebration. A young woman shows the others a park she's been practicing in, her friends start using the installations there in a new way; they bring their perspectives, their skills, their sensitivities, their energy. The young woman rediscovers a landscape she believed she already knew, and her next workout, even if she is once again alone, will gain freshness and pleasure and her imagination will have been surprisingly expanded.

"Even if she is once again alone," the words are banal. But even if it is better to take one's first steps under the supervision of an experienced parkour artist—we're talking about real experience, not a vague collection of skills or a passing fancy—and even if the benefits of sharing experiences and training in groups are many, at times enthusiasts find themselves alone.

It is sometimes only in the zone of day-to-day existence when, having arrived at a certain spot, the practitioner will remember that he or she knows instinctively how to move differently. The childhood spirit suddenly reawakens. Little steps, almost dancing. Well-calculated steps. One or two fun jumps. Touching the material.

But let's look a little deeper into working out by yourself..

Some people choose to work out alone for selfish reasons, others out of arrogance (excessive fear of making mistakes in front of others). Sometimes it's a reflection of a lack of interest in or patience with the brothers and sisters. Fortunately, this is not always the case: for a lot of people, enjoying working on their own is simply a character trait, if sometimes in fact, a noble one; or a manifestation of the neighbours' lack of motivation: even if we promote more active lifestyles, we don't expect everybody in the neighbourhood to train 24/7. Sometimes friends have other things to do, and at other times—and these can be especially rewarding—it is the simple desire to work on variations by ourselves or to tirelessly repeat a specific movement, to fully concentrate on something, to learn something about ourselves that enables us to better internalize the practice. This is essential, at least once you have mastered the basic techniques and safety habits.

It's a question of balance, and therefore of common sense: sharing is vital, and community provides everyone with incredible strength, but at a certain level, we must also learn to be self-reliant. The day when we really need to execute a jump, it is likely that our friends will not be there to cheer us on or give us their opinion on how far the distance is. Solitude is very much part of the practice.

Generally, people are terrified of solitude. They'll do anything to avoid it, preferring bad company to no company at all; if they are confronted with having to be alone, they compulsively launch a series of unsuccessful operations, a bunch of supposedly comforting mini-events that distract them from their true selves. Why this frantic search for artificial security? This way of dealing with boredom is perverse: we definitely want to be happy, but we generate distractions that take us out of the present moment, which alone gives us the possibility of true contentment.

Some cases of twisted logic evaporate as soon as we shine the light of reason on them: we must occasionally contemplate the past and plan for the future, and we are far from advocating an ascetic existence that banishes all fun. The idea is that somebody who cultivates the spirit of chivalry should have no fear of being alone. Especially since the experience of solitude is completely subjective: we may well feel alone in a crowd, just as we can feel connected to life without there being any human presence within the sound of our voice.

A moment of solitude is the very best way to integrate what you've learned and to get up to speed. It is also one of the ideal conditions in which to quickly develop your concentration. While it is essential in parkour to learn to stay focused even when there is noise and pedestrians—after all, it is often the case—it can also be beneficial to find a moment of respite.

Alone, we can repeat the same vault one hundred and fifty times, focusing entirely on a thousand little details, without having to answer to anyone. We can practice a simple movement that would bore our more advanced buddies, spending two hours on the same ramp or railing, or linger on a particularly demanding technique that would discourage beginners. While we are in a creative frame of mind, we can perform a sequence at the speed of a snail, or go flying over the landscape like a gazelle. The way we occupy space and time depends only on us. Alone in the evening, we have the stars for friends and at times the wind as confidant. Alone, our training tends to become more contemplative: we are often more aware of textures, our breathing, the stiffness in our muscles, the sound we make when landing; thus, the impacts of our movements on our body.

These occasional forays into solitude are in any case the lot of anyone who decides to take the path less travelled. As Sébastien Foucan recalled: "Being different often appears to reject being with everyone else, but it isn't rejecting their way—it's looking for your own." [39] We often must make sacrifices, and we can't always do what we like, however we must not lose our integrity and change all our plans in the sole purpose of avoiding solitude. [40]

A phrase an enthusiast will often hear is "alone in the jump." Explicitly, these words remind us that, in a jump, our safety depends on our own skills. The term does not refer exclusively to risky jumps, but applies to all the aspects of the practice. In everything we do, we must learn to be masters of our own bodies, to carry ourselves correctly, in short, to take ownership. Friends inspire us and the environment is not without influence, but we are the ones who make the decisions, and we are the ones who decide how to move. Not the other guy, not the obstacle.

This is a most delicious paradox. We are responsible for our persons, and it is possible to say that we are basically alone with ourselves. And yet, in the next chapter we will see how we are ... never, ever alone.

# X. Compassion
# and Courage

"Self-centeredness inhibits our love for others, and we are
all afflicted by it to one degree or another. For true happiness
to come about, we need a calm mind, and such peace of
mind is brought about only by a compassionate attitude.
How can we develop this attitude? Obviously, it is not
enough for us simply to believe that compassion is important
and to think about how nice it is! We need to make a con-
certed effort to develop it; we must use all the events of our
daily life to transform our thoughts and behavior."

XIVth Dalai Lama, Tenzin Gyatso,
*The Compassionate Life* [41]

**W**e actually can coexist with our fellow human beings in
harmony. Real friendship is a force, a refuge, a source
of inspiration. More than that: our happiness undeniably
depends on others. This is not a mantra, a doctrinaire idea
or a hollow concept. If we carefully study the question, we

realize that in fact all of the qualities that lead to fulfillment—think of love and tolerance, but also qualities such as patience, the queen of virtues since it enables the achievement of all the others—can only develop in relation to other people. The true masters of all traditions speak of this constantly, many books are devoted to it and I myself have written in more detail about it elsewhere. [42] Without an ounce of interest in other people and without an open mind, there's not much in life that's worth pursuing. On the other hand, people who have learned to be open will not be devastated at the first setback, they'll know how to take as much air as they need to breathe, to let things come and go. A big heart is infinitely rich, and a person with genuine compassion has already learned more than the most studied egocentric. The good news is that there are ways to cultivate compassion. [43]

This is one of the great things about group training, as long as it is structured and everybody contributes. We learn to accept ourselves and to appreciate our differences as much as our similarities. I may not have a lot of affinity with such-and-such a person, but we already share a common interest. That other guy sometimes tries my patience, but, like me, he gives his best; like me, he's exhausted by this new quadrupedal exercise. Like me, he sweats! Some people are more gifted than others, but everyone has their limitations. Shared effort, personal boundaries and the potential for compassion. Because that's the beginning of genuine compassion: recognizing that the other person is human too, recognizing that every living being seeks happiness and fears pain, even if we sometimes find them awkward or overly rigid in their opinions. Intense shared effort and collective endeavours prepare the ground for this achievement, whether consciously or not. In a previous chapter, we talked about how our conception of the immediate environment tends to change and that if we persevere in training, our perception of other organisms may also need to change. Over time, we come to realize that there's movement everywhere and at all times, and that no one is completely alone. No one is excluded from the world of the living.

But words are only words. "So try to describe the taste of a papaya or another exotic fruit to a friend," said the master. The exercise of thinking has its limits. So, let's move. Let's give ourselves the experience of moving, give ourselves the experience of this great sharing of energy.

Use all the words that you want, but for those who want to learn to socialize, a few training sessions in parkour will be more profitable.

One of the mottos of the pioneers is *be strong to be useful*. It is a way of giving meaning to training, and even more, to life. Think about it: Be strong to be useful, strength is a means, usefulness is the goal. The idea is to be strong, not to be the strongest; to grow in order to help others grow, to grow without stomping on your neighbour's foot; in short, to keep on learning and to ensure that this learning takes place not only over time but also in the community. Help others become stronger, perhaps even stronger than yourself. It can be simple: generously share your energy while training, do some extra repetitions to finish with the stragglers, bring a little joy and nobility to the city through your everyday behaviour.

But the statement *be strong to be useful* can have more concrete applications. There are many scenarios where endurance, flexibility, agility, coordination, a good sense of balance and other skills can be decisive. What comes to mind most are emergency situations—from the epic confrontations in the myths of antiquity to the many tense incidents of the modern world—where the presence of an athlete is appreciated. This resonates with the legacy of Raymond Belle, David Belle's father: parkour as a survival technique that in some places will be part of the training provided to firefighters and police officers. [44]

Let me be clear though: I'm not talking about playing superheroes, needlessly risking your life or those of others in dangerous exercises, but rather to be of service to others to the limit of our abilities. Be consistent in assessing risk, circumstances and opportunities. Don't confuse courage with madness. For if it's true that every great success begins with a dream, and if so many failures are rooted in timidity, sometimes it's an act of courage and integrity to simply admitting that we have reached our limits. Beyond undertaking spectacular actions, daring to let go of old certitudes can in itself be a heroic act, as recalled so well by Fabrice Midal:

It is not through certitudes that the knight views the world, but through a constant openness of heart and mind. This red-hot vulnerability is essential. To have to be sure we're in the right, to have to be an agent of good, to have no doubt about what we are doing, allows and even invites barbarism. The knight is not always sure to be right, he accepts to live in the midst of uncertainty, since what is good is in the eye of the beholder and changes with the situation. This uncertainty must never prevent us from getting involved: it is on the contrary the source of authentic action. (trans.) [45]

The best action is not always the first right thing that comes to mind. In his book *Budo Secrets*, author, translator, teacher and martial artist John Stevens tells an inspiring story about Jirokichi Yamada (1863-1931), who was a great fencer. [46]

Yamada had received a great many documents on the arts of the sword from his teachers. Feeling as though it was his duty to preserve these veritable gems for future generations, he carefully stored them in a box that could be quickly moved in case of emergency.

The great Kanto earthquake took place on September 1, 1923 causing more than 100,000 fatalities and countless missing. The Kanto plain was devastated, and fires raged in the cities.

Yamada, meticulous though he was, was certainly not aware of such statistics. He took his precious box out of hiding and prepared to flee for safety.

Suddenly, he stopped and thought: "How will it look if people see a samurai running away to protect material possessions! It is foolish to save samurai documents while ignoring the samurai spirit to serve society." He replaced the box and then ran out into the street to help pull people from the rubble and fight the fire. [47]

This is sometimes where courage lies: in accepting the need to review our priorities, to take another look at our opinions. The extent of our courage—and many stories demonstrate this—is greatly increased by compassion. In return, genuine compassion, which is the desire to put an end to all suffering, gives a sense of purpose to the training and infuses the warrior with incredible energy. Solidarity and universal responsibility, strength and courage, selflessness and true happiness: in parkour, everything is related. But the powerful energy that is the result should be used wisely, and that's the topic of the next chapter.

# XI. Humour and Wisdom

"Think lightly of yourself and deeply about world affairs."
Miyamoto Musashi [48]

In the same way that a bird cannot fly with only one wing, compassion, if it is not accompanied by wisdom, will be futile. Conversely, a remarkable intelligence mired in self-centeredness can bring about horrors, as history has witnessed. The parallel with parkour seems remote, but let's dig a little deeper.

We saw in the last chapter that the practice of parkour offers a wonderful opportunity to socialize with those with whom we train and that, more generally, the discipline invites everyone to open to the world. This opening is first manifested by an increased attention to spaces, structures and the immediate environment, but from there to providing benevolent attention to other people, whoever they may be, is only one step. Only one step, or for some, a running jump, but moving from one perception to the other is possible, as are skilful sequences between different vaults.

But people who feel compassion for the suffering of their fellow human beings want to do something to address the problem as soon as possible. This is where discernment and critical thinking make a difference: we need to assess problems, anticipate solutions, estimate how and when to act and have enough objectivity to determine whether we are, or are not, competent enough to remedy the situation. It is important to be passionately engaged, but at the same time avoid drowning in a torrent of emotions and risk embarking on a series of ill-considered actions. A friend is suffering from depression, how can we help? We walk down the street and hear a cry of distress from the second floor of a building, can we really reach the balcony or the window, and is it really desirable?

When we talk about openness, affection or compassion, we must nevertheless keep in mind that our contribution to the city or the community may seem trivial but may actually be essential. In fact, anyone who does his or her job, whatever it is, with good and noble motivation contributes to the equilibrium of the world. Business leaders who respect the environment and human values, people who make health or teaching a vocation, artists who help us rediscover beauty where we had ceased to perceive it, and everybody else, as long as their hearts are true. What is more touching than a baker who does his or her job with love, serving customers with a heartfelt smile? The customers then begin their day on the right foot, so to speak, and it's impossible to quantify the power and influence of moments of human connection.

It would seem to be a truism that the best way to help others find happiness is to be happy yourself. That's not a selfish approach: if you want to repair your neighbour's shoes effectively, you first need to learn basic shoemaking. But unless you're ok with wrecking somebody's Jimmy Choo's, learning "on the job" might not turn out so great. It's just an example. You don't have to have perfect mastery of a field before you dare to practice it, and in any vocation in life we keep on learning. The history of martial arts, Zen and the different traditions contains many examples where teachers and disciples learned from each other. This is precisely the case with parkour. Humility, openness, confidence and the desire to go further all come into play.

This, of course, does not mean that we can do anything at any time, regardless of our level of competence or incompetence. Striking a balance is key, and what immediately comes to mind is the adage *be strong to be useful.* Which is why we train, and why we are constantly learning.

Maintaining this balance is only possible if we avoid falling into useless asceticism and ill-conceived austerities. One way to avoid these pitfalls is to keep your sense of humour.

We're not talking about endless wisecracks or sarcastic insults, or never being able to be serious. The kind of humour we're talking about consists of staying cool in the face of uncertainty, taking pleasure in our imperfections, letting go of our obsessive need to control everything in our own and other people's lives, in short, keeping things in perspective and accepting them how they are, being truly loving. Mischievousness can occasionally be a sign of exquisite freedom! But mean-spirited humour just shows a lack of love for life, or a lack of confidence; and lazily repeating trivialities shows disrespect for the value of people's time. Compassionate humour, combining humility and letting go, is a sign of maturity, while insolence and indolence are just childish.

The kind of healthy humour inherent in parkour is in any case a strong ally that guards against boredom and the tendency to overtrain, eases tension at appropriate moments, shakes us out of our ways of thinking and softens what can be overwhelming fear, shows a bit of self-respect and infuses our comrades with energy. What's more: it enables us to express a bit of audacity and stimulates our creativity.

You have to start with the basics, and only then can you involve your imagination and develop your own moves and style. But when we talk about creativity in parkour, a lot of people only think about the technical aspect (how to do a particular vault, a certain kind of jump). But creativity is also important in terms of conditioning. We must train in such a way that our body gradually adapts to different surfaces instead of just repeating the same exercises in the same places; to repeat what we said earlier, maintaining the functional anatomy by doing simple movements but in a variety of ways to cultivate a love of effort and to avoid falling into monotony.

New ideas can be discovered by folding a contemplative walk into your next work break. Open your eyes, attentively explore the city and its parks. Touch things, live and breathe. Constraints, provided they are healthy, also tend to stimulate the imagination, as is the case in other artistic fields. Simply put, we try to find more and more original ways to get out of the fix we're in. How can you get to the other side without stepping on those stones? And if that railing was red-hot and you could put your feet there for a second, but not your hands? How could you pass efficiently between those two bars if your right arm was broken? In any case, creativity in parkour is not so much measured by the new spectacular moves you worked so hard to discover as it is by figuring out how to string together the movements you have learned—simple though they may be—and possibly finding yourself truly flowing through your environment. This ease is optimal when it becomes instinctive.

However, so that our instincts stay on track, in other words, that we are not fooled by our minds, we must also train them to become wiser. We mentioned above that compassion needs to be combined with discernment; insight is also essential when it comes to our own training.

What do we mean by wisdom? The term does not refer only to theoretical knowledge such as whether or not we know how to speak Esperanto, or how to recognize different kinds of wood turpentines. It is, in short, to perceive reality as it is: to understand at the very least the broad outlines, the "mechanical" foundation, without bringing prejudices, our wild guesses, our intellectual chatter or our emotional gibberish into play. It's basically taking off our blinders.

It's no easy thing, being human! It wasn't easy for the great philosophers and teachers who came before us. But even though this book is not meant to be a philosophical treatise, I would like to focus here on two key steps that can nourish the thinking of anyone seeking freedom. The movement of ideas or the movement of the body ... it might seem bold to compare a physical activity to philosophical thought. We deliberately decided not to dwell too much in this chapter on the links between these two disciplines, preferring to let the reader draw his or her own conclusions. How does contemplating the preciousness of human existence improve my training? What is the connection between this kind of meditation and preventing injuries? What is the relationship between the few minutes I take every day for quiet reflection and my enjoyment in sweating an ocean of salt water doing quadrupedal movements? Specifically, what effect will my meditation on death have on my next running jump or my next arm jump from a height? On the importance I attach to aesthetics, on how I channel my energy and free up my creativity? What makes someone a good practitioner? And—for those who choose this path—a good teacher?

These questions would seem to be of particular significance for parkour artists.

Let's begin by reflecting on the precious nature of human existence. Human life has an incredible potential for freedom, for perfection. No other species has the ability to wake up one morning and decide to become better and stronger. We alone have this freedom. As His Holiness the Dalai Lama points out, a rabid animal can hurt a few people, but a malicious human being can cause infinitely greater harm. Conversely, a dog may under exceptional circumstances save the life of a toddler, but only human beings can consciously devote their lives to the good of others. In short, we have the invaluable opportunity to achieve both material and spiritual goals. We must contemplate this opportunity again and again; we must rejoice in it and make a firm decision to use our intelligence and our time wisely: to use our energy in a constructive way, in a way that conforms to our values. Otherwise, we are like the beggar who is unaware of the ingots of gold bullion buried under his hut.

The transitory nature of things is our second topic of discussion. As Matthieu Ricard writes:

What is the use of reflecting on the transitory nature of beings and things? Human life has incalculable value, but it doesn't last forever. Reflecting on impermanence makes us realize the value of time. Each moment of life is so precious! Yet ordinarily we let it slip away like gold dust between our fingers. Why do we constantly put off until later what we intuitively know is of the highest importance? There's no point jumping up and down with impatience to get results as fast as possible, but we do need to develop an unshakable determination not to waste our time on distractions that make no sense. We must stop being taken in by the illusion that we have our whole life before us. Every moment of this life is precious, because death is certain and could occur at any time. [49]

Many people deliberately avoid thinking about death. Many demonstrate denial, anger, misunderstanding. Many even develop twisted philosophies such as "since life is short, we must make the most of it," thus rationalizing everything from trivialities to so-called extreme experiences. Yet in this there is no lasting satisfaction, and it is reminiscent of a man dying of thirst gulping down seawater.

Thinking about death doesn't have to be morbid. It might even be the best tribute to life, since it is in seeing that our time is limited that we can come to want to use it well. We need to let go of our attraction to the daily trivia that usually clutters our minds and devote more time to what's essential. Thinking about death serves as a catalyst and can provide us with amazing energy. An indispensable step towards lucidity, and thus towards authentic happiness, it can be a surprising source of joy. But this kind of realization does not happen without effort. It is not enough to think about it once and understand something intellectually, you have to understand it in your gut, so to speak, and it takes time and repeated contemplation.

Meditation on death can and should generate three conclusions: 1) death is inevitable, 2) the time and circumstances are completely unpredictable and 3) at the time of death, what really matters is the direction we have given to our existence, and the great human values that we have been able to develop.

Thinking about impermanence while reflecting on the preciousness of human existence can lead to unexpectedly powerful insights, if we've meditated correctly. It's challenging at first, but it can help us become less complicated and a lot calmer. Practitioners of parkour can benefit from the exercise:

it helps us reset our priorities and begin trading our illusions for clarity and madness for true courage. The idea is not to become more fearful; on the contrary, the reflection helps us to take useful and calculated risks and to avoid doing stupid things that we might come to bitterly regret. It gives stability to training, provides a reason for learning. Without any insight, enthusiasm can wane. A reflection on the nature of life—at once temporary and precious—combined with humour and compassion, can bring about real inner change over the long haul and provide practical wisdom and lasting joy.

# XII. Expand your Horizons and Contribute to the Discipline

"Energy is contagious. Catch it, and pass it on!"

Sébastien Foucan, *Freerunning: The Urban Landscape is Your Playground* [50]

"Fight discrimination by setting an example, with intelligence and education."

One of the precepts of the *Yamak Spirit.* [51]

It should be among the priorities of practitioners to avoid turning parkour into a product. Leave the mythmaking, improvised philosophies and urban legends to people who don't practice parkour. Think of how martial arts have become all the rage on the big screen. There are many career opportunities in parkour, and there will soon be many more than we can imagine, but we must not lose sight of the essence of the discipline.

One way to stay grounded would be to occasionally reflect on the definition of "useful," in the precept *be strong to be useful.* Inspiration could be found in the Buddhist essential practice called "the dedication of merit." In this practice, we contribute or share with others the positive benefits generated by our meditation and actions, thus increasing the positivity and happiness in the world. In the Tibetan tradition in particular, the dedication is expressed through a series of wishes for enlightenment and peace in the world, made at the end of any meditative practice. We're not advocating any particular spiritual path; it's just one example of how we can work our training into our personal life.

With this in mind, practitioners must understand that there is a diversity of viewpoints and approaches. Sensitivities, abilities and goals differ, and so does practice.

There are basically two ways to see parkour:

1. As something organic, a constantly evolving whole
2. As a specific legacy to conserve.

Each of these perspectives has its advantages, and each carries risks. In the first, if there is a lack of vigilance, the definition of the practice may become increasingly blurred to finally dissolve into a great "anything." Parkour would then become a bizarre concoction with no structure or rules, an undrinkable soup in which you have mixed together all kinds of ingredients without regard to purpose, and we will have lost sight of the value of training. In the second approach, the practice can become sterile and lacking in creativity; it could become joyless; and in the long run, it would be impossible to cope with new challenges since it had failed to adapt. In one approach there are too many possibilities and we lose our bearings; in the other, too few and we forget the point of what we're doing. Taken to their extremes, such perspectives are always sources of conflict and stagnation. Both can be counterproductive.

So we need to find a third solution, which, without falling into the trap of over-conceptualizing (as that would definitely influence the way we move), we can avoid the pitfalls of both approaches while retaining their positive sides.

First, let's take stock of the positive elements; let's dissociate the various positive elements from these approaches and then take another look. If an approach invites us to be conciliatory, to whom or to what must we direct this spirit? Do acrobatics, for example, have their place in parkour? To what extent and why? Let's ask ourselves these questions, and at the end of the exercise, we might arrive at something like the following:

- Be open (always respect other people)
- Be diligent (in your own training).

  Or, put differently:

- Be demanding of yourself (without being too severe)
- Seek conciliation with other people (without losing your own identity).

  This could be, for some:

- Closely adhering to the aspects of traditional practice while respecting people who express themselves through deliberately aesthetic choices.

  Or for others:

- Always seeking out and opening yourself to new ways of doing things while respecting those who follow the already established paths.


In either case, the idea is to recognize and encourage sincere efforts. Thinking along these lines makes it possible to find a middle way that resonates both authenticity and solidarity. If pleasure is part of the mix, then learning and training will be sustainable over the long haul.

A famous proverb says, "Waves come and go, but the ocean remains." It seems all the more relevant in today's world, where information travels at a phenomenal rate. This proverb is a great help when considering, say, yoga, martial arts, Zen, each of them a "phenomenon" at one time or another, and yet essentially timeless. Parkour has created, creates and will create waves, and occasionally some rather impressive tidal movements. In times such as these, we must remember that the best way to contribute to the discipline is still to live it. To live it, for sure, but according to one's personality, therefore, by internalizing the practice. To do this, we must not hesitate to simplify when the need arises, and contemplate the example of teachers who often speak of returning to the source. It is said that practicing parkour is basically about learning how to interact with the world around us. This is another way of saying that living parkour is primarily about learning to be authentically yourself.

Vincent Thibault
Paris and Québec, 2010-2013

# Appendices

The appendices include an article entitled "Parkour and Web 2.0: Make sure not to get caught in the web," and two lists of precepts or points summarizing the philosophy of the practice, the first by Sébastien Foucan and the second by the Yamakasi and the ADD Academy. They could have just as easily evoked the 21 Precepts of Miyamoto Musashi,[52] the famous swordsman and Zen artist, or other jewels of the great human traditions. However, as pointed out by the authors of *The Ultimate Parkour & Freerunning Book*,[53] the suggestions and philosophies of the founders of the discipline do not constitute rules that are to be followed blindly, but reflect basic positive approaches that invite each person to enter into reflection and discussion. This book is my participation in this discussion.

# APPENDIX 1

## Parkour and Web 2.0
### Make sure not to get caught in the web

It seems imperative to talk about the current drift experienced by the world of parkour.

It's common for people to decide to get involved after having seen videos on the Internet. The fact that parkour videos are attracting interest isn't the problem; on the contrary, we can't figure out everything on our own, and it's good to expose ourselves to ideas that have come to us from around the world. But here we must be wary of two major problems.

The first refers to the current state of the virtual world. A principal characteristic of what is called Web 2.0 is that unlike how things were not so long ago when most media content was produced and distributed by professional organizations (advertisers, businesses, governments, official associations, etc.), now audiences are coveted (and, to some extent, won over) by users, that is to say by individuals. The prominence of YouTube and other video-hosting sites where anyone can post their own video is a good example. In short, users interact with the content of websites, but also with each other. It's a form of natural evolution that involves the sharing of information, with all the beneficial and toxic effects. The first hurdle to overcome, therefore, for anyone who has been introduced to parkour through videos plucked indiscriminately out of cyberspace is precisely that it is easy to pick up bad information. It's often text: dubious stories of superhuman feats, new urban legends, romantic ideas about the origins of parkour, sketchy advice on what to eat before or after training or on what stretches would be best and generalized rundowns on how to diagnose and treat sports injuries. But it is just as often images, such as the numerous videos wherein young people can be seen showing off, shamefully calling what they are doing "parkour." Admittedly, there is a whole lot of whatever out there.

There are any number of these tutorials, these so-called guides to learn this or that parkour move, many of them just disseminating nonsense, not always easy to spot for those who lack experience. (Some guides, rare though they are, are nevertheless very well done. Our friends at UrbanCurrent in Hawaii, for example, have produced some.) Other young people are making videos without claiming to offer parkour lessons but there are inevitably viewers who take them as such, and try to reproduce the movements, which may not always be well executed. The fact is that the brain is capable of recording a surprising amount of information, and we are entitled to wonder whether we always understand what we have seen. Even unconsciously, by dint of seeing poorly executed movements a number of times, enthusiasts can replay them in their heads, imagining themselves performing them. The risk of developing bad habits seems real. Even more serious is the risk of injury (and often bad habits and injuries are related).

Even if web surfers don't have any ambition *to learn* parkour moves from amateur videos, there is always the possibility that they'd like to find a *definition* of parkour. But unless people happen across a very well-written and authoritative account, it is unlikely they'll get a clear idea of what this discipline really is. Why should we train at parkour instead of, say, go to the gym? As practitioners, it is important to ask the question. We need to find out who we are, to understand our identity. To affirm ourselves. This isn't always easy, even after years of training.

Which brings us to the second problem we discussed earlier, the second possible pitfall for those who discover parkour on the web. This is both a matter of the discipline's reputation and the enthusiast's safety. It even goes to the heart of parkour's future. The problem here is that when you see well-executed moves in these video clips, you don't see the work that came before. It is possible that the person who did the move on the video did not succeed the previous two thousand times, or could be hurt the next time. (It is even possible that he was injured at the time, and the watchful eye will see that bad landings and joint impact are all too common.) Even if he or she is a professional and capable of nailing the same move twenty times in a row, the video clip doesn't show the training that preceded it. A well-rounded and challenging training program for the most part executed daily over a period of years, where we not only work on technique, but also skills such as balance and coordination, and where we patiently develop our physical conditioning (which is not just a question of strengthening muscles, but also preparing tendons and ligaments). Injuries are inevitable if we ignore these steps.

As human beings, it is our right to express ourselves. This is one of the favourite themes of parkour, which is itself both a cry for and a celebration of freedom. If you want to make videos, make them, but do it for the right reasons. A priori, there are two (professional portfolios and movies aside). The first is to pay tribute to the discipline, to share what it really is, to dispel the myths held by the general public, or to inspire established practitioners. To do this, you need at least a minimum of video editing, simply to set the context. The second reason would be to teach, either to create a how-to-do-it guide (knowing that nothing beats an instructor in the flesh), or to video yourself in order to better understand your mistakes. In the latter case, there's no point in posting it online; if you need feedback from your colleagues, you can simply give them access to the video by invitation only, or at the very least add a clearly worded warning so that net surfers can understand the context.

It is a little sad to feel the need to write all this since the content should be a matter of common sense. We could have written the same words about a great many subjects, but it seemed all the more imperative since the practice of parkour may entail injury and since the subject suffers from widespread misunderstanding. Let's facilitate healing on all levels! Everyone has the right to learn, everyone has the right to express themselves. We must at all costs preserve these rights, but we must also be vigilant and show consideration for others. For the Internet user—for everyone, in fact—the point is to provide the informational basis and encouragement for critical thinking. Practitioners of parkour need to constantly question the relevance of their approach, seeking the best ways to showcase the discipline and to share its energy with other practitioners, and society in general.

Vincent Thibault
Québec and Paris, 2010

# APPENDIX 2

## The Values of Freerunning According to

### Sébastien Foucan and Freerunning Academy

- Follow your way
- Always practice
- Respect others in their practice
- Be an inspiration for others
- Be positive and look for positive environments
- Respect your environment
- Feel free to try other disciplines
- Don't take it too seriously
- The journey is more important than the goal
- There is no good or bad, right or wrong, but what is important is what you learn from experience through practice
- Freerunning is not an elite discipline, but for people who love to move and keep moving
- Channel your energy in a good way, a way to be better

*Freerunning is more than a physical discipline. It's reclaiming our heritage, relearning what we have forgotten.*

Adapted from: www.foucan.com

# APPENDIX 3

## The "Yamak" Spirit as defined by the

### Yamakasi and ADD Academy

Yamakasi is an African term (Lingala) which means strong man, strong body, strong spirit. This is the name that the original pioneers of the movement chose to give their group.

The Yamak spirit represents the essence of the effort to uphold the values that united the founders of Yamakasi in their pursuit:

- To perceive life as a personal adventure and to respect human beings.
- To respect one's body by healthy nutrition, rest and training.
- To respect nature by simple "green" acts.
- To confront the unknown in order to grow.
- To pursue freedom of thought in order to act.

- To assert oneself in order to take action in the world.
- To fight discrimination by setting an example, with intelligence and education.

Translated and adapted from www.add-academy.com

# Notes

1. Fabrice Midal. *La Voie du Chevalier: dépassement de soi, spiritualité et action* (abridged and revised version of the book published under the title *L'esprit de la chevalerie*). Paris: Payot et Rivages, 2009, p. 14.

2. Nicolas Boileau, also known as Boileau-Despréaux (1636-1711), French poet, author and critic. *The Art of Poetry, Canto I.* The extract precedes the famous lines: "What we conceive, with ease we can express; Words to the Notions flow with readiness." Boileau Despréaux, Nicolas, 1636-1711. *The Art of Poetry.* London, 1683. Accessed online from the Electronic Text Center, University of Virginia Library.

3. Matthieu Ricard (born in 1946), scientist, writer, photographer, Buddhist monk, the Dalai Lama's interpreter and promoter of humanitarian projects to which he has dedicated all his royalties. *Happiness: A Guide to Developing Life's Most Important Skill.* New York: Little, Brown and Company, 2003.

4. Haruki Murakami (born in 1949), Japanese writer, known for among other things, *The Wind-up Bird Chronicle, Kafka on the Shore* and *What I Talk About When I Talk About Running.* The quote is from *1Q84: Book 1.*

5. Muriel Spark (1918-2006), novelist, short story writer, poet and biographer of Emily Brontë and Mary Shelley, who lived in Scotland, England, Rhodesia (now Zimbabwe) and Tuscany. *The Prime of Miss Jean Brodie,* first published in 1961. The quote is from the version published by Everyman's Library, 2004, and accessed online from Google Books.

6. Dugpa Rimpoché, *Préceptes de vie*, translated into French from the Tibetan by Jean-Paul Bourre. Paris: Presses du Châtelet, 1996, p. 69.

7. Shawn Micallef, *Stroll: Psychogeographic Walking Tours of Toronto*, illustrations by Marlena Zuber. Toronto: Coach House Press, 2010. See also *Spacing Toronto: Understanding the Urban Landscape* (www.spacingtoronto.ca).

8. Dr. Julie Angel is an independent filmmaker whose essay on parkour, *Parkour Research: The positive potential, PK4Life,* was published online on April 3, 2011, at www.julieangel.com. See also *Ciné Parkour: A PhD Thesis* (London, 2011) and *The History of Parkour* (London, 2012).

9. *Génération Yamakasi: vol au-dessus des cités*, a 71-minute film by Mark Daniels, coproduced by Api Productions and Majestic Force, with the collaboration of France 2, Planète and Planète Choc, available on DVD from TF1 Vidéo, 2005.

10. *Jump! London*, a documentary directed by Mike Christie and produced by Optomen Television, originally broadcast on Channel 4 in September 2003.

11. Nicolas Bouvier (1929-1998), Swiss writer, photographer, iconographer and traveller. *La Guerre à huit ans et autres textes*, cited by Christine Jordis in the preface of *Œuvres* in the Quarto collection. Paris: Gallimard, 2004, p. 7.

12. David Belle says that he learned a lot from his father, Raymond Belle. For Raymond, parkour was truly a matter of survival. He always questioned the usefulness of a particular training or a particular movement. He wasn't seeking a certain body image, rather the most complete mastery of his body and the power to make optimal use of it when needed. See David Belle, *Parkour*, text and interviews by Sabine Gros La Faige. Paris: Intervista, 2009.

13. Robert Lee Frost (1874-1963), American poet. The extract cited is from the anthology *Mountain Interval*.

14. Bruce Lee (1940-1973), martial artist, director, actor, producer, writer and philosopher. See *Tao of Jeet Kune Do*. California: Ohara Publications, 1998, p. 27 (*Everyday Opportunities for Exercises*).

15. André Van Lysebeth (1919-2004), *Yoga Self Taught*. York Beach, Maine: Red Wheel/Weiser, 1999.

16. *Génération Yamakasi: vol au-dessus des cités*, written and directed by Mark Daniels, *op. cit.*

17. This idea of imagination echoes the previous chapter, Finding the Magic in Everyday Life. Imagination is conceived of in its broadest sense, related to creativity, openness, acceptance, daring, inspiration and therefore to joy.

18. Lawrence Block (born in 1938) is a well-known mystery writer. The paraphrase is from *Telling Lies for Fun & Profit: A Manual for Fiction Writers*. New York: William Morrow, 1981 and 1994. Chapter 21: *Burning the Raft at Both Ends*.

19. For an introduction to the beneficial effects of exercise on emotional health, see *Guérir: le stress, l'anxiété et la dépression sans médicaments ni psychanalyse* by Dr. David Servan-Schreiber. Paris: Robert Laffont, 2003, subsequently revised. Chapter 10, Prozac ou Adidas?, is dedicated to the benefits of sport.

20. Trungpa, Chögyam. *True Perception: The Path of Dharma Art*. Boston: Shambhala Publications, Inc., 2008, p. 125.

20. André Comte-Sponville (born in 1952), French philosopher. See, among his numerous works, *A Short Treatise on the Great Virtues*. New York: Henry Holt and Company, 2001, accessed online from Google Books. The extract cited comes from the first chapter on Politeness.

22. Yamamoto Tsunetomo (1659-1719), *The Book of the Samurai*. New York: Kodansha America, Inc., 2002, p. 41.

22. See the short video *Parkour on Guam (Respect ParkOUR Environment)*, published on the Urban Current from Hawaii Parkour, and the *Leave No Trace* initiative started by Parkour North America members.

24. *Génération Yamakasi: vol au-dessus des cités,* written and directed by Mark Daniels, op. cit. See also the 26-minute documentary *Grimper aux murs,* directed by Mark Daniels in 2005 and available on the DVD edition of *Génération Yamakasi.* See also the documentary *Jump Westminster* directed by Dr. Julie Angel in 2007.

25. David Belle, *Parkour,* text and interviews by Sabine Gros La Faige. Paris: Intervista, 2009, p. 65.

26. Pema Chödrön (born in 1936), writer and Buddhist nun of American origin, director of the Gampo Abbey in Nova Scotia. *The Wisdom of No Escape.* Boston: Shambhala Publications, Inc., 1991, p. 130.

27. *Jump! London,* documentary directed by Mike Christie, *op. cit.*

28. Christophe André, psychiatrist at L'Hôpital Sainte-Anne, Paris, author of several books on psychology. See *Psychologie de la peur: craintes, angoisses et phobies.* Paris: Odile Jacob, 2004; chapter 1, *Peurs normales et peurs pathologiques,* p. 12.

29. Shantidéva (c. 685-763), *Bodhicaryavatara,* translated by Kate Crosby and Andrew Skilton. New York: Oxford University Press, 1995. Chapter VIII, verses 129-130.

30. The event was called the American Rendezvous and was a seminar with instructors from Parkour Generations (UK) and the ADD Academy (France), organized by Parkour Horizons (U.S.), a tightly knit community of devoted and generous practitioners and instructors.

31. Shunryu Suzuki (1904-1971), a monk of the Soto Zen school, often confused with D. T. Suzuki, and a person who has made a significant contribution to the understanding of Zen in North America. *Zen Mind, Beginner's Mind.* Boston: Shambhala Publications, 1970.

32. Frank Forencich, *Exuberant Animal: The Power of Health, Play and Joyful Movement*. Bloomington, Indiana: Authorhouse, 2006. Highly recommended reading.

33. *Parkour: The Nature of Challenge*, a 37-minute long documentary written by Dave Sedgley, directed by Paul Maunder and produced by Northern Parkour, 2009.

34. Frank Forencich, *Exuberant Animal*, *op. cit.*, p. 54.

35. See for example the excellent documentary *Jump Westminster* by Dr. Julie Angel, 2007.

36. Frank Forencich, *Exuberant Animal*, *op. cit.*, p. 53.

37. ADD Academy (Art Du *Déplacement* Academy): "a global educational program created and developed by Yann Hnautra, Châu Belle and with support from Laurent Piemontesi, Guylain N'Guba Boyeke and Williams Belle (the Yamakasi founders)." See www.facebook.com/addacademy/info.

38. Dugpa Rimpoché, *Préceptes de vie*, *op. cit.*, p. 71.

39. Sébastien Foucan, *Freerunning: The Urban Landscape Is Your Playground*. Berkeley: Ulysses Press, 2008, p. 70.

40. *Ibid.*, p. 82: "Travel together and help each other grow, but don't alter your path just so you have company."

41. XIVth Dalaï-Lama, Tenzin Gyatso. *The Compassionate Life*. Boston: Wisdom Publications, 2003, p. 20.

42. See Vincent Thibault, *Source de bonheurs et de bienfaits: petite introduction au bouddhisme;* Brossard: éditions Un monde différent, 2009; and especially *Quand les sombres nuages persistent: conseils du cœur à ceux qui vivent des moments difficiles et à ceux qui les aiment;* Boucherville: Éditions de Mortagne, 2010.

43. The Tibetan tradition in particular has made the training of the mind to compassion into a science. See in this regard, for example, the works

of Matthieu Ricard, including *Happiness: A Guide to Developing Life's Most Important Skill, op. cit.*, and *On the Path to Enlightenment,* Boston: Shambhala Publications, Inc., 2013.

44. For more on this subject, see David Belle, *Parkour, op. cit.*

45. Fabrice Midal, *La Voie du Chevalier: dépassement de soi, spiritualité et action*, *op. cit.*, p. 79.

46. John Stevens, *Budo Secrets: Teachings of the Martial Arts Masters.* Boston: Shambhala Publications, 2001, p. 104.

47. According to the story told by Stevens, the documents survived unscathed.

48. Miyamoto Musashi (1584-1645) is considered to be one of the greatest swordsmen in history. The precept is drawn from John Stevens, *Budo Secrets, op. cit.;* see also *The Book of Five Rings* in the bibliography and Kenji Tokitsu, *Miyamoto Musashi: His Life and Writings.* Boston: Shambhala Publications, 2004.

49. Matthieu Ricard, translated by Sherab Chödzin Kohn. *Why Meditate?* Carlsbad, Calif.: Hay House, 2010, pp. 42-43, accessed online from Google Books. See also: Vincent Thibault, *Quand les sombres nuages persistent*, *op. cit.*, chapter 3, first section: "Impermanence et possibilités."

50. Sébastien Foucan, *Freerunning, op. cit.*, p. 98.

51. Source: www.add-academy.com (2011); see Appendix 3.

52. See John Stevens, *Budo Secrets, op. cit.*

53. J. Witfeld, I. E. Gerling, and A. Pach, *The Ultimate Parkour & Freerunning Book.* Maidenhead, UK: Meyer & Meyer Sport, 2011, p. 32.

# Bibliography

Alain (Emile Chartier). *Alain on Happiness.* New York: Frederick Ungar, 1978.

André, Christophe. *Psychologie de la peur.* Paris: Odile Jacob, 2004.

Angel, Julie. *Ciné Parkour: A PhD Thesis.* London: Julie Angel, 2011.

Angel, Julie. *The History of Parkour.* London: Julie Angel, 2012.

Arendt, Hannah. *The Human Condition.* Chicago, University of Chicago Press, 1958.

Augé, Marc. *In the Metro.* Minneapolis, Minn.: University of Minnesota Press, 2002.

Belle, David. *Parkour,* interviews by Sabine Gros La Faige. Paris: Intervista, 2009.

Carrio, Christophe. *Un corps sans douleur.* Vergèze: Thierry Souccar Éditions, 2008.

Chödrön, Pema. *The Wisdom of No Escape.* Boston: Shambhala Publications, Inc., 1991.

Chödrön, Pema. *The Places That Scare You: A Guide to Fearlessness in Difficult Times.* Boston: Shambhala Publications, Inc., 2001.

Comte-Sponville, André. *A Short Treatise on the Great Virtues.* New York: Henry Holt and Company, 2001.

Dalaï-Lama, H. H. and Howard Cutler. *The Art of Happiness.* New York: Riverhead Books, 1998.

Day, Andy. *The Moments Between: A parkour road trip through Italy.* Andy Day, 2010.

Deshimaru, Taisen. *The Zen Way to the Martial Arts.* New York: Arkana, 1982.

Edwardes, Dan. *The Parkour and Freerunning Handbook.* London: Harper Collins, 2009.

Forencich, Frank. *Exuberant Animal: The Power of Health, Play and Joyful Movement.* Bloomington, Indiana: AuthorHouse, 2006.

Foucan, Sébastien. *Freerunning: The Urban Landscape Is Your Playground.* Berkeley: Ulysses Press, 2008.

Lee, Bruce. *Tao of Jeet Kune Do.* California: Ohara Publications, 1998.

Midal, Fabrice. *La Voie du Chevalier: dépassement de soi, spiritualité et action.* Paris: Payot et Rivages, 2009.

Murakami, Haruki. *What I Talk About When I Talk About Running: A Memoir.* New York: Vintage Books, 2009.

Musashi, Miyamoto. *Gorin no sho. The Book of Five Rings.* (translation by William Scott Wilson), Boston, Shambhala Publications, 2002.

Ricard, Matthieu. *Happiness: A Guide to Developing Life's Most Important Skill.* New York: Little, Brown and Company, 2003.

Ricard, Matthieu. *Why Meditate?* Carlsbad, Calif.: Hay House, 2010.

Ricard, Matthieu. *On the Path to Enlightenment.* Boston: Shambhala Publications, Inc., 2013.

Rimpoché, Dugpa. *Préceptes de vie.* Paris: Presses du Châtelet, 1996.

Rinpoché, Dzigar Kongtrül. *Le bonheur est entre vos mains.* Paris: NiL Éditions, 2007.

Rivers, Frank. *The Way of the Owl: Succeeding with Integrity in a Conflicted World.* New York: HarperCollins, 1997.

Servan-Schreiber, David. *Guérir: le stress, l'anxiété et la dépression sans médicaments ni psychanalyse.* Paris: Robert Laffont, 2003.

Stevens, John. *Budo Secrets: Teachings of the Martial Arts Masters.* Boston: Shambhala Publications, 2001.

Suzuki, Shunryu. *Zen Mind, Beginner's Mind.* Boston: Shambhala Publications, Inc., 2006.

Thich Nhat Hanh. *No Death, No Fear.* New York: Riverhead, 2002.

Trungpa, Chögyam. *True Perception: The Path of Dharma Art.* Boston: Shambhala Publications, Inc., 2008.

Trungpa, Chögyam. *Shambhala: The Sacred Path of the Warrior.* Boston: Shambhala Publications, Inc., 1984.

Tsunetomo, Yamamoto. *Hagakure. The Book of the Samurai.* New York: Kodansha America, Inc., 2002.

Walker, Brad. *The Anatomy of Sports Injuries.* Berkeley: North Atlantic Books, 2007.

Witfeld, J., I. E. Gerling, and A. Pach. *The Ultimate Parkour & Freerunning Book.* Maidenhead, UK: Meyer & Meyer Sport, 2011.

# About the Author

Vincent Thibault is a writer. He is the co-founder and director of the Académie québécoise d'art du *déplacement* (ADD Academy of Quebec, www.addquebec.ca) and was the first Quebecer to become a certified instructor of parkour, which he learned in France and the United States. Vincent regularly teaches in Quebec City and has led workshops outside of Quebec, including in Asia. He counts among his friends some of the world's authorities on the subject. He is the author of several books, including *La Pureté,* a collection of Japanese-inspired short stories published by Hamac (to be published in English under the title *Purity*), *Les Mémoires du docteur Wilkinson,* a collection of detective stories and *Les Bêtes*, a novel that takes place on a First Nations reserve, both published by Éditions de la Pleine Lune.

For more information: www.vincentthibault.com. You can also follow him on Facebook: www.facebook.com/vincentthibaultdotcom.

ALSO AVAILABLE FROM BARAKA BOOKS

**Fiction**

*The Adventures of Radisson, Hell Never Burns*
by Martin Fournier

*Break Away 1, Jessie on My Mind*
*Break Away 2, Power Forward*
by Sylvain Hotte

*Principals and Other Schoolyard Bullies*
Short Stories by Nick Fonda

*I Hate Hockey*
by François Barcelo

**Nonfiction**

*Challenging the Mississippi Firebombers, Memories of Mississippi 1964-65*
by Jim Dann

*A People's History of Quebec*
by Jacques Lacoursière and Robin Philpot

*The History of Montréal, The Story of a Great North American City*
by Paul-André Linteau

*Slouching Towards Sirte, NATO's War on Libya and Africa*
by Maximilian Forte

*Dying to Live, A Rwandan Family's Five-Year Flight Across the Congo*
by Pierre-Claver Ndacyayisenga

*Soldiers for Sale, German "Mercenaries" with the British in Canada During the American Revolution*
by Jean-Pierre Wilhelmy